ANALYZING THE ISSUES

CRITICAL PERSPECTIVES ON FREEDOM OF THE PRESS AND THREATS TO JOURNALISTS

Edited by Bridey Heing

Enslow Publishing

101 W. 23rd Street
Suite 240
New York, NY 10011
USA

enslow.com

Published in 2019 by Enslow Publishing, LLC
101 W. 23rd Street, Suite 240, New York, NY 10011

Library of Congress Cataloging-in-Publication Data

Names: Heing, Bridey editor.
Title: Critical perspectives on freedom of the press and threats to
  journalists / edited by Bridey Heing.
Description: New York, NY : Enslow Publishing, 2019. | Series: Analyzing
  the issues | Includes bibliographical references and index. | Audience:
  Grades 7-12.
Identifiers: LCCN 2018002108| ISBN 9780766098541 (library bound) | ISBN
  9780766098558 (pbk.)
Subjects: LCSH: Freedom of the press—United States—Juvenile literature. |
  Censorship—United States—Juvenile literature. | Journalism—Political
  aspects—United States—Juvenile literature.
Classification: LCC PN4738 .C75 2018 | DDC 323.44/50973—dc23
LC record available at https://lccn.loc.gov/2018002108

Printed in the United States of America

To Our Readers: We have done our best to make sure all website addresses in this book were active and appropriate when we went to press. However, the author and the publisher have no control over and assume no liability for the material available on those websites or on any websites they may link to. Any comments or suggestions can be sent by email to customerservice@enslow.com.

Excerpts and articles have been reproduced with the permission of the copyright holders.

Photo Credits: Cover, Paul Bradbury/OJO Images/Getty Images; cover and interior pages graphics Thaiview/Shutterstock.com (cover top, pp. 3, 6-7), gbreezy/Shutterstock.com (magnifying glass), Ghornstern/Shutterstock.com (interior pages).

CONTENTS

INTRODUCTION

Democracy relies on many parts of society in order to govern effectively. From the institutions enshrined in the Constitution to the voters who elect representatives, every part has to work together in order to ensure that governance is conducted transparently and with the will of the people behind it. One of the most important parts of any democracy is the press, which acts as a watchdog and source of information, helping keep governments honest and accountable to the people.

Sometimes called the Fourth Estate, the press has a complex role in countries around the world. They are responsible both for ensuring those in power answer to the public and for making sure the public is adequately informed about the goings-on that influence their government. Because of this dynamic, the press and those in power can have a highly adversarial relationship—it isn't rare for the press to spar with authorities, or to be taken to task by those in power for crossing what some see as lines in the name of a story.

But around the world, the press is under threat. Governments that do not want to answer to the people often target the press for restriction or even assassinations in a bid to silence those who would speak out against injustice. Elsewhere, including the United States, rhetoric from those in power is seen as a danger to journalists, who are cast as enemies of the state. The rise of fake news and the appearance of partisanship among media professionals has also given rise to a diminishing of the role of the press in protecting democracy; as a result, many feel the press is a nuisance or actively working against the best interests of the country.

Threats to journalists and dangers to the freedom of the press have serious ramifications for democracy. It makes it harder for the Fourth Estate to play the role they have been playing for centuries—namely, that of guardian over the relationship between the elite and those whom the elite govern. Without a free and trusted press, a link between the government and the people, which is meant to bring to light injustice as well as highlight the good work government can do, is effectively broken. Without that link, democracy becomes all the more precarious.

This collection will look at threats to freedom of the press around the world, from the perspective of academics, governments, average citizens, and those on the front lines of the fight to ensure press safety. While global in scope, the central question of what role the press plays in democracy—and what is lost when freedom of the press is threatened—will be answered in a way that applies to all countries, and highlights the importance of the Fourth Estate.

CHAPTER 1

WHAT THE EXPERTS SAY

The media and democracy are deeply intertwined, making it nearly impossible to study one without considering the other. In strong and ideal democracies, the press is free from intimidation or influence, able to report on the goings-on of state without fear. But often the reality of government-press interaction is far more complex, with the state working to obscure or influence the press to varying degrees. This can shift into an outwardly aggressive stance on the part of the government, with experts pointing at obstruction of the press as a sign of a weakening or even collapsing democracy. In these essays, experts examine the ways in which government and the press interact, and what correlations exist between democratic states and freedom of the press.

"STOP THE PRESSES," BY JOHN FEFFER, FROM *FOREIGN POLICY IN FOCUS,* OCTOBER 12, 2016

Imagine that Donald Trump wins the presidency. Then, as he has done throughout his career, he goes after his enemies. He purges the Republican Party of everyone who refused to support him. He initiates criminal proceedings against Hillary Clinton.

And he shuts down *The New York Times* and *The Washington Post.*

It sounds like an unlikely scenario. Even if he does somehow manage to pull his campaign out of hospice to win in November, Trump wouldn't be able to just close the leading newspapers in the United States, however much he might despise the liberal media.

But that's exactly what's happening elsewhere in the world. In Hungary, Viktor Orban's government this week pulled some strings behind the scenes that led to the shuttering of the leading daily newspaper, Nepszabadsag. Earlier this year, the government of Recep Tayyip Erdogan closed one of the top Turkish papers, *Zaman.* In Russia back in 2008, someone — perhaps a 400-pound guy sitting on his bed — pulled the plug on *Moskowski Korrespondent* after it reported on an affair between Russian President Vladimir Putin and a 24-year-old gymnast.

Welcome to the brave new world of censorship. Today's illiberal democrats pretend to respect press freedom. But they don't tolerate any criticism that threatens their political and economic position. They'll throw individual journalists in jail. But they're also not above muzzling an entire paper. At a time when corporate pressures threaten press diversity and reporters in many countries risk their lives to pursue leads, the latest attacks on the media by corrupt populists are contributing to a global rollback of fundamental rights.

ATTACKING THE PRESS

Every year Reporters Without Borders puts out a survey of press freedom. Its 2016 report, issued in April, was the grimmest yet. Last year showed nearly a 4 percent decline in freedom of the press globally, according to their metric, and a 13 percent deterioration since 2013.

The many reasons for this decline in freedom of information include the increasingly authoritarian tendencies of governments in countries such as Turkey and Egypt, tighter government control of state-owned media, even in some European countries such as Poland, and security situations that have become more and more fraught, in Libya and Burundi, for example, or that are completely disastrous, as in Yemen.

One key statistic for measuring press freedom is the number of journalists in jail, which dropped very modestly last year (from 221 in 2014 to 199 in 2015). But 2016 looks as though it will easily exceed the record. Turkey alone has 120 journalists in jail, 70 of them on charges related to the failed coup in July. China, which had the dubious distinction of leading the world in throwing reporters behind bars in 2015, began to crack down harder on journalists and editors in Hong Kong this year. Egypt, Iran, Israel, and Azerbaijan have all been turning the screws on reporters. Even here in the United States, the police have arrested or harassed citizen reporters trying to document police brutality, and Georgia is attempting to prosecute a woman who did nothing more than record a public rally put on by the state Republican Party.

But why go after single reporters when you can shut down an entire newspaper? That's certainly been the approach of Turkish President Recep Tayyip Erdogan, whose evolution from reformer to reactionary has been dramatically accelerated by his heavy-handed approach to the press.

His move against *Zaman* in March, however, repre-sented a new front in the battle.

Zaman was Turkey's largest-circulation newspaper. After initially supporting the Turkish leader and his Justice and Development Party, the daily reversed gears and began to launch investigative probes of Erdogan's polit-ical circle. Like two other previously state-appropriated periodicals, Bugun and Millet, *Zaman* was also linked to the Fethullah Gulen movement (which Erdogan claims was behind the coup). The closure looked like an anti-ter-rorist operation. Using tear gas and a water cannon, the police stormed the building and escorted the editor and his colleagues out of the building. Shortly thereafter, a new pro-government edition of *Zaman* appeared. In the wake of the attempted coup in July, Erdogan closed the paper for good, along with a slew of Gulen-linked media outlets, including 45 newspapers, 16 television stations, 23 radio stations, and 15 magazines. Last month, the government closed another 20 radio and TV stations, many of them connected to ethnic Kurds.

Though he claimed that *Zaman* supported the "terrorist" Gulen faction, Erdogan was also angered by the paper's 2013 investigation of high-level corruption that involved money-laundering and fraud associated with an oil deal with Iran. The Turkish state went after *Zaman* not only to prevent it from publishing news about current affairs but also to eliminate its version of history. The authorities wiped clean the newspaper's archives, consigning all 27 years of articles to the dustbin. The government that controls the past can control the future.

Just this week, Viktor Orban achieved the same goal in Hungary but through different means. He didn't send police into the offices of *Nepszabadsag*. But the Hungarian government managed to use its political influence behind the scenes to silence a paper that in its final editions exposed the corrupt dealings of the governor of the Central Bank, a major embarrassment for Orban's Fidesz government. The ruling party then had the gall to pretend in its official announcement that it was respecting, not undermining the rule of law: "The suspension was a reasonable business decision rather than a political one. It would be in violation of the freedom of the press if we interfered with a decision of a media owner."

Nepszabadsag, once the official newspaper of the Communist party and then relaunched under the ownership of the Socialist Party, was Hungary's largest daily. So, the economic argument rings hollow. Even the far-right-wing party Jobbik, which has found common cause with Fidesz on a number of issues, didn't fall for Orban's ploy. "The total undermining of *Népszabadság* is the latest example of Viktor's Orbán's megalomania," a Jobbik spokesperson said. "The only aim of Fidesz is to either gain 100% control over Hungarian media or to obstruct it."

Until relatively recently, Hungary had one of the most vibrant and interesting media landscapes in the region. Yet in a mere six years, since the beginning of his first term in office, Orban has bulldozed that landscape, leaving behind only monuments to himself and his party. The EU is not likely to do anything — its past condemnations of Orban's illiberal policies may well have increased his stature inside the country. It's up to Hungarians themselves to reclaim their country.

Hungary and Turkey are not alone. The year has been full of newspaper seizures. South Sudan shut down a newspaper for reporting on the corruption of government officials. Oman did the same thing in August to a newspaper reporting on corruption in the judiciary. The state of Jammu and Kashmir in India banned the local paper, *Kashmir Reader*, for "disturbing the peace," but really because it was reporting on the growing unrest in the province.

It's striking that corruption is the common denominator behind many of these newspaper closures. Despite their appeals to nationalism or religion or some political ideology, the new illiberal leaders have been singularly focused on using the apparatus of the state to enrich themselves and their followers. Since their political opposition has often indulged in the same illicit activities, only the press and a few organizations devoted to transparency stand in the way of what political scientists call "state capture."

CORPORATE CONCENTRATION

Newspapers are closing in the United States all the time, though for different reasons. The latest casualty is the *Pittsburgh Tribune-Review*, leaving the western Pennsylvania city with only one daily. Last spring, *The Tampa Tribune* bit the dust. There are now fewer than a dozen two-paper towns in the United States. As many publications move online, the age of daily print journalism is winding down.

At the same time, the media landscape has become ever more concentrated. In 1983, 50 corporations controlled 90 percent of U.S. media. Now that number has dwindled to a mere six corporations.

Sure, you can find on the web a few islands of investigative journalism and provocative alternative opinion (in an ocean of outlandish conspiracy theories). But what Orban and Erdogan are doing consciously in Hungary and Turkey is happening as a result of market calculations here in America.

Of course I'm a big fan of online media. And I've indulged over the years in plenty of critiques of mainstream media. But independent journals of record, with budgets for investigative journalists and fact-checkers, are indispensible in holding elected leaders accountable. These are the bloodhounds who can really follow the money. But substantial news outfits are in a losing battle for readers with clickbait operations like BuzzFeed.

In mid-August, Donald Trump showed both his ignorance of and contempt for the press when he tweeted: "It is not 'freedom of the press' when newspapers and others are allowed to say and write whatever they want even if it is completely false!"

Actually, that's exactly what freedom of the press is. It's not up to Trump or Orban or Erdogan to decide what is "completely false." That is up to the fact-checkers, the courts, and ultimately, the dwindling group of citizens around the world who care passionately about politics and truth, those two often incommensurate categories that are, rather than the "elite," the real target of Donald Trump's crusade.

1. What is freedom of the press, according to this article?

2. How do governments restrict freedom of the press, and why?

"FLOGGING FOR BLOGGING?" BY MEDEA BENJAMIN, FROM *CODE PINK*, JANUARY 14, 2015

On January 9, two days after the massive Paris march condemning the brutal attack on freedom of the press, a young Saudi prisoner named Raif Badawi was removed from his cell in shackles and taken to a public square in Jeddah. There he was flogged 50 times before hundreds of spectators who had just finished midday prayers.

Those 50 lashes — labeled by Amnesty International a "vicious act of cruelty" — were the first installment on his sentence of 1,000 floggings, as well as 10 years in prison and a fine of $266,000.

Badawi's crime? Blogging.

The father of three young children, Badawi hosted the website known as Free Saudi Liberals, a forum intended to promote a lively exchange of ideas among Saudis. Badawi wrote about the advantages of separating religion and state, asserting that secularism was "the practical solution to lift countries (including ours) out of the third world and into the first world." He accused Saudi clerics and the government of distorting Islam to promote authoritarianism. And unlike the Saudi rulers, Badawi cheered the Egyptian uprising against Hosni Mubarak, calling it a decisive turning point not only for Egypt but "everywhere that is governed by the Arab mentality of dictatorship."

In mid-2012, Badawi was arrested for his blogging and accused of ridiculing the kingdom's religious police, the Commission for the Promotion of Virtue and Prevention of Vice. He was also charged for failing to remove "offensive posts" written by others. The prosecution originally called for him to be tried for "apostasy," or abandoning his religion, which carries the death penalty.

If nothing changes, Raif Badawi will be flogged every Friday for the next 19 weeks. And he will not see his wife or children — who were forced to flee to Canada to avoid public harassment at home — for 10 years.

Badawi's case is not unique. In 2014, Reporters Without Borders described the Saudi government as "relentless in its censorship of the Saudi media and the Internet," ranking Saudi Arabia 164th out of 180 countries for freedom of the press.

Last year, four members of the Saudi Civil and Political Rights Association, an organization documenting human rights abuses and calling for democratic reform, were sentenced to prison terms ranging from 4 to 10 years. The fourth member sentenced was Omar al-Saeed, who was handed four years in prison and 300 lashes because he called for a constitutional monarchy.

Or look at the case of another human rights lawyer, Walid Abu al-Khair, in prison since 2012. On January 13, a Saudi court increased his prison term from 10 to 15 years after he refused to show remorse or recognize the court that handed down his original 10-year term for sedition. Al-Khair, founder of the Monitor of Human Rights in Saudi Arabia (MHRSA) and legal counsel for blogger Badawi, was convicted on charges of disrespecting King Abdullah and the Saudi authorities.

Saudi Arabia also remains the only country in the world to maintain a ban on women drivers. According to this law, women are strictly restricted to the passenger seat of vehicles. This ban is so harshly imposed that two women — 25-year-old Loujain al-Hathloul and 33-year-old Maysa al-Amoudi — were not only arrested for driving to the United Arab Emirates, but they were also referred to be tried by a terrorism court. In the past, punishments for women drivers have included loss of jobs, passport revocation, and even floggings.

The U.S. government's response to these egregious and inhumane punishments from its ally usually takes the form of a State Department spokesperson expressing "concern." But there is no major public condemnation. No threats of cutting arms sales. No sanctions against government officials. The U.S. government basically turns a blind eye to the medieval forms of torture the Saudis still mete out.

One major reason is oil. Since before World War II, the United States has viewed Saudi Arabia as a strategic source of petroleum. In 1933, the Arab American Company (ARAMCO) was established as a joint venture by both countries. Currently, Saudi Arabia is the second largest supplier of petroleum to the United States.

With the money it receives from oil, the Saudi government purchases vast amounts of weaponry from the United States. In 2010, the U.S. government announced that it had concluded a deal to sell $60 billion of military aircraft to Saudi Arabia — the largest U.S. arms sale deal in history. One use of U.S. tanks was seen in Bahrain, where the Saudis intervened to crush a democratic uprising against the Bahraini monarchy.

There's now congressional legislation being introduced to declassify a 28-page section of the 9/11 commission report that allegedly exposes the direct role of the Saudi government in the Twin Tower attacks on 9/11.

After all, Saudi Arabia supplied 15 out of the 19 9/11 hijackers and was the home of Osama bin Laden. The country exports a radical version of Sunni Islam, Wahhabism, that fuels extremism throughout the Middle East. It treats its women as second-class citizens. And it's the world capital of beheadings, with the government carrying out 87 public beheadings in 2013 and at least nine already this year.

Being a top oil provider does not give a country the right to dehumanize its own people. The United States is certainly no model for respecting freedom of expression — as we saw in the streets of Ferguson, where peaceful protesters were teargassed and beaten — but it shouldn't overlook the human rights abuses carried out by an allied country that imprisons, tortures, and executes its citizens simply for speaking their minds.

So take a moment to call the Saudi Embassy in Washington, DC (202-342-3800, then press "3" for the Public Affairs office) and tell them "Free speech is not, and should never be, a punishable crime. *Je suis Raif!*"

1. Do other countries have a responsibility to protect freedom of the press in foreign states?

2. Why did the Saudi government target a blogger?

"IS FREEDOM OF THE PRESS REQUIRED FOR A LIBERAL DEMOCRACY?" BY JOSHUA BARETT, FROM *MAPPING POLITICS*, FALL 2014

[Editor's note: Tables are not included in this reproduction, but can be found with the original article.]

ABSTRACT

Democracies within states have become more predominant than at any other point in history. Whether this shift is directing towards liberal democracies, however, has yet to be determined. This article focuses on freedom of the press and how it is required for a liberal democracy. Using Mexico as a case study, this paper identifies how a state is unable to excel in its democratic principles without the virtues of a free press. Using the Freedom House dataset, countries are categorized by their level of democracy against their level of free press. Although Mexico holds many democratic values, this paper concludes that a country cannot be truly democratic without adequate freedom of the press.

INTRODUCTION

Freedom of the press is central to liberal democracies throughout the world. Limpitlaw (2011) defines liberal democracy as a representative democratic government which operates under the tenants of liberalism such as protecting the rights of individuals; free, fair, and competitive elections between multiple distinct political parties; a separation of powers between different branches of government; and the equal protection of civil liberties and political freedom from all individuals. A free press allows media, such as radio, television, or print, to relay information to citizens, put pressure on governments, and hold governments accountable. However, in some cases (such as Rwanda), media has been used as a deterrent to promoting freedom and democracy within a state. This paradox raises important questions over whether a free press is always a positive feature of democratization. To answer this question, this paper uses a comparative analysis to examine information on countries provided by Freedom House to determine if there is a relationship between media rights and democracy. It also provides an explanation as to why certain countries, such as Mexico, do not have laws to protect freedom of the press but are seen as democratic states. This paper concludes with a discussion of how freedom of the press can positively influence democracy.

METHODOLOGY

To address the central question of the relationship between free press and democracy two fundamental methods are used in this paper. First, information was drawn from Freedom House's data set on 2013 freedom of the press. Freedom House is an independent organization that is dedicated to expanding freedom around the world. Their mission is to influence democratic political environments so that governments are accountable to their people, that the rule of law prevails, and the rights of women and minorities are guaranteed (Freedom House, 2013b). It is a reputable organization that initiates programs and provides reports on democracy levels around the world, gathering data for key democratic indicators such as religious freedom, media freedom, and elections.

The other dataset for the comparative assessment was obtained through The Economist Intelligent Unit's (EIU) 2012 Democracy Index (2013). As a British organization, EIU has provided research and analysis of economies around the world for the past 70 years. One drawback with using EIU's dataset is their adherence to a certain ideology while ranking economies, such as neoliberalism. They still, however, provide significant contributions to the work on democratization and the global economy and are respected and frequently used by scholars such as Sarah Cook, Arch Puddington, and Vukasin Petrovic (Freedom House, 2013b). This paper categorizes data in a comparative study to determine the cases that may undermine the theory of free press (Diamond, 1999; Park, 2002; and Williams and Pavlik, 1994) positively correlating with a liberal democracy. Table 1 is divided into 3 columns including country, freedom of the press, and level of democracy. In the freedom of the press column, countries are ranked from 1 to 3. A country with a free press is ranked as 1 because a free press plays a key role in sustaining and monitoring the democracy of a nation, which contributes to the overall accountability of a government. A non-free press is ranked as 3 because a country without a free press represses the views of individuals that attempt to provide outlets for governments to be accountable. Finally, a partly free press (ranked as 2) lies somewhere in the middle where governments provide some access for media, but continue to play an active role in limiting media rights (Freedom House, 2013b).

Similarly, the level of democracy is divided into four categories: full democracies (ranked as 1), flawed democracies (ranked as 2), hybrid regimes (ranked as 3), and authoritarian regimes (ranked as 4) (Diamond, 2002). The EIU states that, "the Democracy Index is based on five categories: electoral process and pluralism; civil liberties; the functioning of government; political participation; and political culture" (EIU, 2013). Although ambiguous, the assumption is that a full democracy portrays these attributes consistently throughout the facets of their state, whereas an authoritarian regime neglects any or all of these aspects.

KEY FINDINGS

Based on this analysis, there are two key findings that warrant further discussion; countries that rank high in both democracy and free press, and countries that rank high in democracy but low in free press. All 25 countries listed as full democracies (1) were also listed as having free media (1). The 16 other countries listed as having full freedom of press were only listed as flawed democracies (2), the second highest score a state could receive (these are highlighted in dark grey in Table 1). There were no hybrid regimes (3) or authoritarian regimes (4) that correlated with having full freedom of press. In four cases, states actually received a higher score in their level of democracy than their freedom of press. Malaysia, Mexico, Paraguay, and Thailand were all ranked as flawed democracies (2), yet they received the worst ranking available for freedom of press – no freedom (3) (these are highlighted in light grey in Table 1). This clearly contradicts the belief that freedom of press is necessary for promoting democracy. The Democracy Index 2012 report (2013) indicates the rankings of democracy in countries Mexico, Thailand, Malaysia and Paraguay as 51, 58, 64, and 70, respectively. Mexico is viewed as the most democratic between the four countries, yet it does not have adequate provision of media. Given this paradox, it will be highlighted as a case study in the following section.

CASE STUDY: MEXICO

Mexico is an intriguing case to examine for many reasons. When compared to the United States and Canada, Mexico is often viewed as a poor state. The country is, and has been dealing with violence, drugs and corruption for many years. The economic development of the country historically has not yielded substantial optimism for a prosperous future. Despite this, there are many indicators that show how Mexico is shifting towards a full democracy and enhancing its clout as a powerful state in the years to come.

In 2000, Vincente Fox, leader of the National Action Party (PAN) was voted to office through democratic elections, ending the Institutional

Revolutionary Party's (PRI) 71-year dominance. This regime haunted the country for decades as it engaged in many authoritative principles (Reséndiz, 2006). However, with the PRI defeat, the country has gradually adopted more democratic principles. In 2006, PAN was re-elected to office, winning by a narrow margin over the Party of the Democratic Revolution (PRD). The 2000 and 2006 elections indicate Mexico has ended its history of one party rule with several parties now engaged in the democratic process (ibid).

Mexico's economy is also rapidly growing. As of 2012, it was the tenth largest oil producer and the largest silver producer in the world. Economists consider Mexico as a regional power, middle power, an emerging power, and a newly industrialized country (Scott, Hau, and Hulme, 2011; Bozyk, 2006). It also has the fourteenth largest nominal Gross Domestic Product (GDP) and the tenth largest GDP by Purchasing Power Party (PPP) with GDP valued at 1.186 trillion USD in 2012 – more than doubling its GDP level in a span of thirteen years (World Bank, 2012). Some believe that by 2050, Mexico will be among the fifth to seventh largest economies in the world (PwC Economics, 2013).

Mexico has also been investing in their health care sector and education systems in recent years. Beginning in the early 1990s, Mexico entered a transitional stage in health care, resulting in medical infrastructure in the major cities being upgraded to similar standards as developed nations (World Bank, 2012). Similarly, literacy rates have soared since the Mexican Revolution, with rates of over 97% for youth under 14 and 91% for people over 15 (ibid). Universidad Nacional Aut Autónoma de México is also ranked 190th in the top 200 World University Ranking as of 2009 (Symonds, 2009). These indicators show Mexico is shifting towards a more liberal democracy.

Even with Mexico's shift towards a liberal democracy, it continues to be one of the most dangerous places in the world for journalists (Freedom House, 2013a). In many cases, governments have threatened – or as some speculate, killed – certain individuals in the media that write in favour of the opposition. Moreover, drug cartels continue to play an active role in influencing and corrupting the government and local businesses (Cevallos, April 2014). Cevallos further argues:

> In the last seven years in Mexico, 35 journalists were killed and six went missing, 84 media workers filed complaints of insults or attacks in 2007, and in the first few days of 2008, the prestigious independent radio commentator Carmen Aristegui, who has often criticized the powers that be, was fired. Given that outlook, many analysts wonder whether the media in Mexico is really as free as the government of conservative President Felipe Calderón claims.

Despite the fact that media personnel are being killed because of their work, Articles 6 and 7 in the 1917 Mexican constitution guarantees freedom of the press. However, even after Mexico's declaration of independence, the traditional practices of government controlling the press are still evident. Mexican broadcasting is not completely commercial, but rather includes a mix of both private and public companies (Schneider, 2011). Due to the long reign of the PRI, the state and the private sector were able to make long-term relationships to develop private broadcasting companies. The situation became more politically heated in the 1960s, when the government signaled a takeover of broadcasting service. After several broadcasting companies merged, Televisa, a private company won the battle over the monopoly of media in Mexico. In spite of this, Televisa continued to have a strong relationship with the PRI, allocating 80 percent of their election coverage to the party compared to granting PAN only three percent of airtime (Schleicher, 1994). Given these examples, it appears as though democracy was struggling to develop during the PRI regime.

To determine if the relationship between freedom of the press and democracy illustrated in Mexico is present in other jurisdictions it is useful to examine a second state. Malaysia is approaching a liberal democracy, yet does not have a free press to determine if the results are consistent. The country holds elections every five years to select a new government; their GDP has been growing 6.5% on average for close to 50 years; and their education rates are well above average (FITA, 2006). However, the government and political parties own most of the country's newspapers, and current legislation creates numerous restrictions for knowledge dissemination (Ahmad, 2010). Unfortunately, even with Malaysia progressing towards a liberal democracy, their lack of a free press hinders their ability to become a true liberal democratic state. This parallels with the findings in Mexico as both countries struggle to provide freedom of the press in their jurisdictions.

ANALYSIS: DOES FREEDOM OF THE PRESS INFLUENCE DEMOCRACY?

Mexico is a unique example as it is taking significant steps towards becoming fully democratic state, yet it lacks appropriate laws for media freedom. A major issue in Mexico is the interdependence between politics and media, whereby the mass media market is highly concentrated and is arguable the most concentrated private sector system in the world (Hughes and Lawson, 2005). As noted above, having a concentration in media leads to skewed airtime when it comes to politics and advocates issues that benefit certain parties.

While the changes in media may not occur in the next few years, there is optimism for the future. It is important to remember that Mexico is shifting towards a democracy and not authoritarianism. The change of government in 2000 ushered in the development on new media legislation, including the 2003 bill, "The Federal Law of Transparency and Access to Public Government Information" (Schneider, 2011). It also renewed Article 41 of the constitution in 2007, which removed the rights of any political parties to buy airtime on radio or television (ibid). While it is clear that there is much work to be done in promoting freedom of the press in Mexico, it appears the country is moving towards an independent and free press.

As depicted in the case study and Table 1, there is a relationship with freedom of the press and fully democratic countries (Williams and Pavlik, 1994). From this perspective, it would appear that freedom of the press does positively influence democracy.

There are several reasons that explain this connection. It is believed that citizens of a nation that vote in elections must be informed of the issues at hand, the candidates that are running for office, and the right to participate freely in public discourse (Limpitlaw, 2011). Having media outlets that skew information by perpetuating governmental bias may not appropriately deliver the information registered voters need to make informed decisions. This goes against one of the underlying attributes of a democracy: that people have a right to elect a government, where part of the right is to understand who they are voting for (ibid).

The press can also play the role of an advocate for democracy and good governance. In many situations, the press will show how the decisions of the government can improve or worsen the life of ordinary citizens. Media can report on not only what is happening, but also what should be happening. This is important, especially for developing nations, as decisions made by an authoritative figure or party can play a direct role in improving basic human living conditions. Pressures exerted by the press can help provoke optimal solutions. There are many ways the press can influence democracy in this capacity. For example, the media can identify which authorities are using clean administration versus corruption and nepotism, appropriate use of public resources versus mismanagement and waste, as well as other areas (Bratton, 1994).

Lastly, and most importantly, the press can act as a catalyst for democracy and development. Even if the press is only able to authentically perform the most basic function of reporting on the matters of public interest, it is still acting as a promoter of transparency, openness, and accountability. The 2002 World Bank president, James Wolfensohn, expresses in a report that:

> A key ingredient of an effective development strategy is knowledge transmission and enhanced transparency. To reduce poverty, we must liberate access to information and improve the quality of information. People with more information are

empowered to make better choices. For these reasons I have long argued that a free press is not a luxury. It is at the core of equitable development. The media can expose corruption. They can keep a check on public policy by throwing a spotlight on government action. They let people voice diverse opinions on governance and reform and help build public consensus to bring about change (2002: 14).

Acknowledging these points, it is evident that the provision of media does positively influence democracy. Mexico has made a powerful pursuit in becoming a more democratic country. However, they can never be truly democratic unless they allow media to report on controversial ideas without repercussions.

CONCLUSION

Although today's world may not be dominated by democracies, it has the largest percentage of states that are in the transitional stages of becoming democratic than ever before (EIU, 2013). As this paper has described, freedom of the press is a significant right when becoming democratic. Without exception, if a state has full freedom of the press, they are either a full or a flawed democracy. The case of Mexico depicts the recent trend the country has been following to initiate democratic principles throughout their policies and practices. However, without appropriate media rights to advocate controversial and oppositional views, a state cannot be an authentic democracy. Therefore, the provision of media does influence democracy, and flawed democracies working towards obtaining media rights are moving in the right direction.

1. What role does the press play in liberal democracies?

2. According to these findings, can a democracy be strong without freedom of the press?

"MAKING MEDIA ACCOUNTABLE TO THE PUBLIC BOLSTERS PRESS FREEDOM," BY DENIS MULLER, FROM *THE CONVERSATION*, FEBRUARY 3, 2015

Julian Disney, the outgoing chair of the Australian Press Council, made a singularly powerful argument in his valedictory speech to the National Press Club on Wednesday: that freedom of the press is strengthened, not weakened, by effective public accountability.

Discussing press freedom, Disney said: "The council's main and unique contribution to the cause of press freedom is its core work of developing standards of media practice and responding to complaints about possible breaches."

In doing so, Disney put his finger on something that the media industry is unwilling or incapable of accepting: press freedom ultimately depends on public legitimacy, and that legitimacy rests in part on public accountability. The industry's attitude to this was vividly illustrated by its reaction to the Finkelstein inquiry into press regulation in 2012. Finkelstein and others who espoused the view that there should be meaningful media accountability were Stalinists bent on censorship.

As Disney also recounted, the spectre of external regulation – as Finkelstein recommended – spooked the newspaper companies into boosting their funding for the Press Council. At the same time, they also agreed to set funding levels at least three years in advance, to give four years' notice of any intention to withdraw from the council and to remove themselves from membership of the complaints adjudication panels.

Set against the troubled history of the Press Council – littered with arbitrary withdrawals of membership and cuts to funding, threatened and actual – these seemingly modest achievements are quite significant. They reflect not only the pressure brought about by the Finkelstein inquiry, but Disney's robust and determined leadership.

Over the past two years in particular, Disney has endured a sustained and highly personalised campaign by News Corp against his chairmanship. That company's newspapers took to calling the Press Council "Disneyland" as they ridiculed and misrepresented Disney's reforms.

Disney named no names in his speech, but the target of some of his remarks was clear to anyone who has followed the history. For example, when speaking about the Press Council's independence and integrity, he said:

> Above all, the council must not be diverted from meeting the responsibilities that it, including its major publisher members, has solemnly assured the public it will fulfil. If honouring these commitments meets fierce attack from a powerful voice

or voices in the industry, the council will need to continue standing firm.

Potential estrangement or loss of a dissident publisher, no matter how powerful, cannot justify deceiving the public and disadvantaging the other publishers who will continue to respect council processes and decisions, even when not agreeing with them.

In a similar vein, Disney had this to say about freedom of speech:

> The freedom should not be largely the preserve of powerful interests in government, business or the ranks of publishers. These powerful interests also should not use their freedom of speech to gravely damage – even destroy – other people's freedom of speech.

It was especially important that freedom of the press was not abused by, for example, repeatedly and seriously misrepresenting what a person had said, or by abusing or intimidating a person with whose views it disagreed. Disney said:

> If a publication repeatedly and flagrantly engages in these kinds of practices, can it credibly portray itself as a supporter of free speech? Or is it only a supporter of free speech for people with whom it agrees or from whom it seeks support?

News Corp will not like this, nor will it like Disney's advocacy of a series of reforms that it continues to oppose. Among them is the increased use by the Press Council of the power to investigate possible serious breaches of its standards even when there has been no specific complaint, but where it is important to clarify publicly whether there has been a breach.

There was a strong case to do this in the aftermath of the Lindt Café siege in Sydney in December 2014. Among some otherwise excellent media coverage, there were some serious breaches of privacy, exemplified by the exploitation of people's Facebook content.

Respect for privacy has been one of the priority issues for the Press Council under Disney's chairmanship. He spoke of the increased threats to privacy arising from digital technology:

> There is a common belief in the media that if a photograph is taken in or from a place to which the public has access, there is necessarily no breach of privacy. But the true test is whether the relevant place and activity meant that the person had a reasonable expectation of privacy.

Consistent with this view, Disney has presided over – and driven – the development of a new set of specific standards to flesh out the Press Council's general principles. One was concerned with the protection of hospital patients from media intrusions; another was on the coverage of suicides.

Work has started on the burgeoning conflicts of interest arising from so-called "content marketing" or "native advertising", where paid advertising is embedded and disguised in what appears to be news content.

So, as Disney acknowledged, there is still much to do. For all its weaknesses, the Press Council is the best

Australia has by way of an accountability mechanism for newspapers. He leaves it noticeably stronger than he found it.

Disney's calls for further reform deserve to be heeded with the same determined sense of purpose he brought to the job.

1. How can the press be held accountable to the public?

2. Why is it important that the press fulfill its obligation to the public?

CHAPTER 2

WHAT THE GOVERNMENT AND POLITICIANS SAY

The government and the press often have a complex relationship, one that hinges both on the press reporting on the goings-on of the state and revealing actions that are antithetical to democracy. But most politicians respect and understand the importance of a free press for a functional state and reaffirm their support for the Fourth Estate. This can, however, be undermined by legislation that does active harm to the press or blocks access to meaningful political decisions. Understanding this dynamic can be difficult, but it is critical to recognizing the ways in which the state can infringe on the rights and activities of journalists, both at home and abroad.

"SCHIFF, PENCE LAUNCH CONGRESSIONAL CAUCUS FOR FREEDOM OF THE PRESS," FROM THE OFFICE OF ADAM SCHIFF, HOUSE OF REPRESENTATIVES, MAY 3, 2006

Washington, D.C. - In honor of World Press Freedom Day, Representatives Adam Schiff (D-CA) and Mike Pence (R-IN) today kicked off a new bipartisan, bicameral caucus aimed at advancing press freedom around the world. The Congressional Caucus for the Freedom of the Press, co-chaired by Reps. Schiff and Pence in the House and by Senators Chris Dodd (D-CT) and Richard Lugar (R-IN) in the Senate, creates a forum to combat and condemn media censorship and the persecution of journalists around the world.

"A free and open press is vital to a healthy democracy. Journalists should not have to work in fear of governments throwing them in jail or harming them or their families simply for doing their job," Schiff said. "By raising awareness of media censorship around the world, this caucus aims not only to protect journalists from persecution, but also to defend citizens' access to unfettered information."

"Where there is no freedom of the press, there is no freedom," Pence said. "If America is to be a beacon of hope to the world, we must hold high the ideal of a free and independent press, advance it abroad and defend it at home. I am honored to associate myself with the men and women in Congress in both parties who advocate the freedom of the press for all of mankind."

Although international law clearly guarantees freedom of expression and the right to a free press, these rights continue to be violated on a broad scale everyday. In 2005, more that 65 journalist were killed, 1,300 physically attacked or threatened, and thousands imprisoned, just for doing their jobs. In light of these increasing attacks on free expression and the lives of journalists, the Caucus will work to raise awareness of threats to press freedom and to journalists working in dangerous countries and conditions.

- The Congressional Caucus for the Freedom of the Press will advance press freedom protect journalist through the following initiatives:
- Convene experts to discuss the status of press freedom in "hot spot" countries to raise awareness of these issues among Members of Congress and the general public;
- Acquire and assemble reports on the incidence and prevalence of media censorship and journalist mistreatment and the services and supports available to victims of persecution;
- Initiate letters and petitions in support of organizations and campaigns for enhanced openness and tolerance in the press in order to advocate justice for murdered or imprisoned journalists;
- Provide guidance to Congress and federal agencies on policies and actions related to press freedom at home and abroad
- Recognize the courageous dedication of individual journalists who are reporting on important developments around the world, often at great personal and professional risk.

The following organizations welcomed the establishment of the Congressional Caucus for the Freedom of the Press: the Committee to Protect Journalists, Reporters without Borders, Freedom House, the Reporters Committee for Freedom of the Press, Free Press, the Newspaper Association of America, the National Endowment for Democracy, the Daniel Pearl Foundation, the Robert F. Kennedy Memorial.

Congressman Schiff is a former Assistant U.S. Attorney in Los Angeles and is a member of both the House Judiciary and International Relations committees. He represents California's 29th Congressional District, which includes the communities of Alhambra, Altadena, Burbank, East Pasadena, East San Gabriel, Glendale, Monterey Park, Pasadena, San Gabriel, South Pasadena and Temple City.

Congressman Pence is in his third term in Congress, representing Indiana's 6th Congressional District. He is a former radio talk show host and practicing attorney. He serves on the Judiciary, International Relations and Agriculture Committee.

1. What is the goal of the Congressional Caucus for the Freedom of the Press?

2. Why, according to those who founded it, is this caucus important?

"H. R. 2242 - WORLD PRESS FREEDOM PROTECTION ACT OF 2015," FROM THE UNITED STATES CONGRESS, MAY 5, 2015

To protect the internationally recognized right of free expression, ensure the free flow of information, and protect journalists and media personnel globally.

IN THE HOUSE OF REPRESENTATIVES

MAY 5, 2015

Mr. Smith of New Jersey (for himself, Mr. Blumenauer, and Mr. Pitts) introduced the following bill; which was referred to the Committee on Foreign Affairs, and in addition to the Committees on the Judiciary and Ways and Means, for a period to be subsequently determined by the Speaker, in each case for consideration of such provisions as fall within the jurisdiction of the committee concerned

A BILL

To protect the internationally recognized right of free expression, ensure the free flow of information, and protect journalists and media personnel globally.

Be it enacted by the Senate and House of Representatives of the United States of America in Congress assembled,

SECTION 1. SHORT TITLE.

This Act may be cited as the "World Press Freedom Protection Act of 2015".

SEC. 2. DEFINITIONS.

In this Act:

(1) APPROPRIATE CONGRESSIONAL COMMITTEES.—
The term "appropriate congressional committees"
means—

(A) the Committee on Armed Services, the
Committee on Financial Services, the Committee on Foreign Affairs, the Committee on Homeland Security, and the Committee on the Judiciary of the House of Representatives; and

(B) the Committee on Armed Services, the
Committee on Banking, Housing, and Urban
Affairs, the Committee on Foreign Relations,
the Committee on Homeland Security and
Governmental Affairs, and the Committee on
the Judiciary of the Senate.

(2) FOREIGN PERSON.—The term "foreign person"
means an individual who is neither a citizen or
national of the United States.

SEC. 3. AUTHORIZATION OF IMPOSITION OF SANCTIONS FOR RESTRICTIONS ON THE RIGHT TO THE FREEDOM OF EXPRESSION AND RESTRICTIONS ON JOURNALISTS.

(a) In General.—The President may impose the
sanctions described in subsection (b) with
respect to a foreign person if the President
determines, based on credible information,
that the foreign person—

(1) is responsible for severe restrictions on the freedom of expression or freedom of the press, including the arrest, harassment, torture, mistreatment, threats, fines, or the pervasive surveillance of journalists, blockage or censorship of the Internet that hinders the free flow of information from journalists, or other serious violations of the international right to the freedom of expression; or

(2) has materially assisted, sponsored, or provided financial, material, or technological support for, or goods or services in support of, an activity described in paragraph (1) .

(b) Inadmissibility To United States.—The sanctions described in this subsection are the following:

(1) ineligibility to receive a visa to enter the United States or to be admitted to the United States; or

(2) if the foreign person has been issued a visa or other documentation to be used to enter the United States, revocation, in accordance with section 221(i) of the Immigration and Nationality Act (8 U.S.C. 1201(i)), of the visa or other documentation.

(c) Consideration Of Certain Information In Imposing Sanctions.—In determining whether to impose sanctions under subsection (b), the President shall consider—

(1) information provided by the chairperson and ranking member of each of the appropriate congressional committees; and

(2) credible information obtained by other countries and nongovernmental organizations that monitor violations of human rights.

(d) Waiver For National Security Interests.— The President may waive the application of subsection (b) with respect to a foreign person if the President determines that such a waiver is in the national security interests of the United States.

(e) Exception To Comply With United Nations Headquarters Agreement.—Subsection (b) shall not apply to a foreign person if admitting the foreign person into the United States is necessary to permit the United States to comply with the Agreement between the United Nations and the United States of America regarding the Headquarters of the United Nations, signed at Lake Success June 26, 1947, and entered into force November 21, 1947, and other applicable international obligations of the United States.

(f) Termination Of Sanctions.—The President may terminate the application of sanctions under subsection (b) with respect to a foreign person if the President determines and reports to the appropriate congressional committees not later than 15 days before the termination of the sanctions that—

(1) credible information exists that the foreign person did not engage in the activity for which sanctions were imposed;

(2) the foreign person has been prosecuted appropriately for the activity for which sanctions were imposed; or

(3) the foreign person has credibly demonstrated a significant change in behavior, has paid an appropriate consequence for the activity for which sanctions were imposed, and has credibly committed to not engage in an activity described in subsection (a) in the future.

(g) Regulatory Authority.—The President shall issue such regulations, licenses, and orders as are necessary to carry out this section.

SEC. 4. REPORTS BY PRESIDENT TO CONGRESS.

(a) In General.—The President shall submit to the appropriate congressional committees an annual report that includes—

(1) a list of each foreign person with respect to which the President imposed sanctions pursuant to section 3 during the year preceding the submission of the report;

(2) the number of foreign persons with respect to which the President terminated sanctions under section 3 during that year;

(3) the dates on which such sanctions were imposed or terminated, as the case may be;

(4) the reasons for imposing or terminating such sanctions; and

(5) a description of the efforts of the President to encourage the governments of other countries to impose sanctions that are similar to the sanctions authorized by section 3.

(b) Dates For Submission.—

(1) INITIAL REPORT.—The President shall submit the initial report required by this subsection not later than 180 days after the date of the enactment of this Act.

(2) SUBSEQUENT REPORTS.—

(A) IN GENERAL.—The President shall submit each subsequent report required by this subsection on December 10, or the first day thereafter on which both Houses of Congress are in session, of—

(i) the calendar year in which the initial report is submitted if the initial report is submitted before December 10 of such calendar year; and

(ii) each subsequent calendar year.

(B) CONGRESSIONAL STATEMENT.—Congress notes that December 10 of each calendar year has been recognized in the United States and internationally since 1950 as "Human Rights Day" and thus the importance of December 10 of each calendar year as the date of submission of the subsequent reports required by this subsection.

(c) Form.—The report required by subsection (a) shall be submitted unclassified form, but may contain a classified annex if necessary.

(d) Public Availability.—

(1) IN GENERAL.—The unclassified portion of the report required by subsection (a) shall be made available to the public, including through publication in the Federal Register.

(2) NONAPPLICABILITY OF CONFIDENTIALITY REQUIRE-MENT WITH RESPECT TO VISA RECORDS.—If the President decides to publish the names of individuals sanctioned in a report required under this section, the President may do so without regard to the requirements of section 222(f) of the Immigration and Nationality Act (8 U.S.C. 1202(f)) with respect to confidentiality of records pertaining to the issuance or refusal of visas or permits to enter the United States.

SEC. 5. LIMITING VISAS TO EXECUTIVES OF STATE-OWNED NEWS AND MEDIA ORGANIZATIONS OPERATING IN THE UNITED STATES.

(a) Policy Statement.—Given the critical importance of the press freedoms and the free flow of cross-border information for diplomatic, political, and financial relations globally, and for purposes of investors, businesses, and politicians making informed decisions, it should be the policy of the United States Government to respond strongly and persuasively to the growing number of restrictions, threats, detentions, harassment, arrests, pervasive surveillance, killings, and delays or denials of visas faced by foreign journalists and their domestic employees, especially the blockage and censorship of the websites of news corporations.

(b) Limitation On I–Visas.—Section 101(a)(15) (I) of the Immigration and Nationality Act (8 U.S.C. 1101(a)(15)(I)) is amended by inserting "subject to section 214(s)," before "upon a basis".

(c) Restrictions On Visas To Executives Of State-Owned Media.—Section 214 of the Immigration and Nationality Act (8 U.S.C. 1184) is amended by adding at the end the following: "(s) Restrictions On Visas To Executives Of State-Owned Media.—

"(1) IN GENERAL.—In the case of an alien who is an executive of a state-owned media organization of a foreign state and is applying for a visa under section 101(a)(15)(I) during a fiscal year, the visa shall be refused if any United States journalist or news organization personnel were expelled, had visas denied, or faced intimidation or violence or other restrictions in the course of working in the foreign state during the previous fiscal year.

"(2) DEFINITION.—For purposes of this subsection, the term 'executive of a state-owned media organization of a foreign state' means a representative, operating in a managerial or executive capacity of a media organization that is majority owned, operated, or controlled by a foreign government operating in the United States.".

(d) Transition Rule.—

(1) IN GENERAL.—The President may order the immediate revocation, delay, or refusal of visas under section 101(a)(15)(I) of the Immigration and Nationality Act (8 U.S.C. 1101(a)(15)(I)) issued to, or sought by, executives of a state-owned media organization of a foreign state before the date of the enactment of this Act in proportion to the expulsions, visa delays or denials, and intimidation experienced by United States journalists or news organization personnel in the course of working in the foreign state during the fiscal year preceding the fiscal year in which this Act is enacted.

(2) DEFINITION.—For purposes of paragraph (1), the term "executive of a state-owned media organization of a foreign state" means a representative, operating in a managerial or executive capacity of a media organization that is majority owned, operated, or controlled by a foreign government operating in the United States.

SEC. 6. INCLUSION OF ADDITIONAL INFORMATION RELATING TO RESTRICTIONS FACED BY JOURNALISTS WORLDWIDE IN THE ANNUAL COUNTRY REPORTS ON HUMAN RIGHTS PRACTICES.

The Foreign Assistance Act of 1961 is amended—

(1) in section 116(d)(12) (22 U.S.C. 2151n(d)(12))—

(A) in subparagraph (B), by striking "and" at the end;

(B) in subparagraph (C), by striking the period at the end and inserting "; and"; and

(C) by adding at the end the following:

"(D) for each country—

"(i) a detailed description of the restrictions imposed against journalists and their domestic personnel, including a description of surveillance, harassment, detentions, death threats or physical attacks, censorship, including on the Internet, denials or delays of visas or travel documents, direct sources of pressure or intimidation, or any other restrictions that limit the ability to report information freely or restricts the free flow of information whether by governments, military, intelligence or police forces or criminal groups, armed extremists, or rebel groups; and

"(ii) a brief assessment of the country's practices with respect to foreign journalists and their domestic personnel by describing the country's practices as 'very restrictive', 'restrictive', 'partially restrictive', or 'mostly free'; and"; and

(2) in the first subsection (i) of section 502B (22 U.S.C. 2304)—

>   (A) in paragraph (2), by striking "and" at the end;

>   (B) in paragraph (3), by striking the period at the end and inserting "; and"; and

>   (C) by adding at the end the following:

"(4) for each country—

"(5)

>   "(A) a detailed description of the restrictions imposed against journalists and their domestic personnel, including a description of surveillance, harassment, detentions, death threats or physical attacks, censorship, including on the Internet, denials or delays of visas or travel documents, direct sources of pressure or intimidation, or any other restrictions that limit the ability to report information freely or restricts the free flow of information whether by governments, military, intelligence or police forces or criminal groups, armed extremists, or rebel groups; and

>   "(B) a brief assessment of the country's practices with respect to foreign journalists and their domestic personnel by describing the country's practices as 'very restrictive', 'restrictive', 'partially restrictive', or 'mostly free'.".

SEC. 7. RESTRICTIONS ON THE FREEDOM OF EXPRESSION AND CENSORSHIP OF THE INTERNET TREATED AS A RESTRICTION ON TRADE.

(a) Finding.—Congress finds that restrictions on the activities of United States journalists and media personnel and the censorship and blockage of websites and the cross-border flow of information damages the competitiveness of United States corporations and limits access to information critical for investors, consumers, and others making market and financial decisions and should be considered a restriction of trade and an unfair competitive advantage benefitting foreign government-controlled news organizations and other news and media corporations.

(b) Statement Of Policy.—Congress declares the following:

(1) The United States Government should seek as part of international treaty negotiations and in negotiations and bilateral discussions with China, Vietnam, Saudi Arabia, and other countries rated "Not Free" by Freedom House's annual "Freedom of the Press" survey, conditions for a free and unfettered operation of websites, an end to visas restrictions for journalists, an end to harassment, intimidation, and surveillance of foreign journalists and an end to the abuse of state secrets laws, including China's restrictions on the sharing of information between Chinese and foreign journalists.

(2) In addition, the United States Government should seek to link expansion of the free flow of information with ongoing and future trade agreements, and other bilateral agreements and communiques, by seeking language eliminating any and all limitations on market access for news agency services and eliminate any restrictions on cross-border data flows involving journalists and the media, including in the Trans-Pacific Partnership, Bilateral Investment Treaties, or any other trade negotiations planned or in progress and seek stipulations guaranteeing fair treatment of United States and other foreign journalists and their publications, consistent with the treatment received by foreign journalists operating in the United States and free and unfettered operation of websites in China and other countries where they are blocked or censored.

(c) Sense Of Congress.—In order to promote freedom of the press and recognize the importance of that internationally recognized right to economic freedom and economic security, it is the sense of Congress that—

(1) restrictions on journalists and media websites and the censorship of the Internet are significant foreign trade barriers;

(2) the United States Trade Representative should include a list of United States websites blocked in foreign countries in reporting on trade barriers in its annual report on foreign trade barriers; and

(3) the United States Government should pursue, at the World Trade Organization (WTO), disputes to end blockage of United States websites by foreign governments, which would include requirements for other members of the WTO to regularly publish a list of any banned or censored websites and provide website owners an opportunity to appeal.

1. Describe the tools this bill allows the US to use against states that hinder freedom of the press.

2. Why does the bill specifically target regimes that restrict access to the internet?

"REMARKS BY THE PRESIDENT ON WORLD PRESS FREEDOM DAY," FROM THE WHITE HOUSE ARCHIVES (PRESIDENT BARACK OBAMA), MAY 1, 2015

THE PRESIDENT: Well, as many of you know, Sunday is World Press Freedom Day, a day in which we reaffirm the vital role that a free press plays in democracy and shining a light on the many challenges, cruelties and also hopeful stories that exist in countries all around the world.

Journalists give all of us, as citizens, the chance to know the truth about our countries, ourselves, our governments. That makes us better. It makes us stronger. It gives voice to the voiceless, exposes injustice, and holds leaders like me accountable.

Unfortunately, in too many places around the world, a free press is under attack by governments that want to avoid the truth or mistrust the ability of citizens to make their own decisions. Journalists are harassed, sometimes even killed. Independent outlets are shut down. Dissent is silenced. And freedom of expression is stifled.

And that's why I really appreciated and valued the opportunity to hear from three journalists who have been incredibly courageous under some very, very difficult circumstances. All three are from countries that severely restrict the freedom of the press. All three have been detained or harassed in the past. All three have sought refuge here in the United States. And we welcome them so that they can continue their important work.

Just very briefly, I want to mention them. We have Fatima Tlisova, who is from Russia. She reported on military operations in the North Caucasus region, as well as disappearances and corruption. She was attacked, kidnapped, tortured herself. Today, she reports for the Voice of America, and most recently has spent time reporting on the Boston trials related to the Boston bombing. So we very much appreciate Fatima being here.

We also have Dieu Cay -- that's his pen name -- from Vietnam, a blogger who has written on human rights, including religious freedom, is a leading voice for greater press freedom in Vietnam. He spent six years in prison and was just released in October.

And finally, we have Lily Mengesha, who is from Ethiopia. She helped to shine a light on the outrage of child brides. After her advocacy for a free press, she was harassed and detained. Today, she is with the National Endowment for Democracy.

So I heard firsthand I think from all of them the importance of all of us, including the United States government, speaking out on behalf of the value of freedom of the press. As I indicated to them, these are countries in which we are engaged and do a lot of business, and we think that engagement and diplomacy is absolutely critical to the national interest of the United States. But what's also important is that we speak out on behalf of the values that are enshrined in our Constitution and our Bill of Rights, because we believe those values are not simply American values, that certain core values like being able to express yourself and your conscience without danger is a human right, a universal right, and ultimately makes the world better and stronger when individual conscience and a press that is free is allowed to function.

It's also a time for us to reflect and honor all those journalists who are languishing in jail as we speak right now, are being harassed, are in danger, and, of course, journalists whose lives were lost. That includes Steven Sotloff and James Foley and Luke Somers; those killed in Paris at Charlie Hebdo. We'll keep working for the release of journalists who are unjustly imprisoned, including Jason Rezaian of *The Washington Post*, who is currently being held in Iran.

So, once again, I want to thank the three journalists who are here for sharing with me in very clear and stark terms some of the challenges that folks are facing. I want everybody to understand that this will continue to be a priority for the United States in our foreign policy, not only because it's the right thing to do, but also because ultimately I believe it's in the national interest of the United States.

So, with that, since it's World Press Freedom Day, I figure I'd better take at least one question.

Q Will the charges against the police in Baltimore, sir, help to defuse things there?

THE PRESIDENT: Before I answer your question, when we were discussing why I thought freedom of the press was so important, I actually used the example of Selma, the incredible courage of those marchers across the bridge, and I pointed out that had there not been good reporters like Mr. Bill Plante at that bridge that day, America's conscience might not have been stirred and we might not have seen the changes that needed to be made. So that's just one example of why press freedom is so important.

Bill, the State's Attorney had literally just walked to the podium as I was coming in here, so I've not had an opportunity to see the nature of the charges. I didn't watch the press conference that she engaged in. So let me just say this, building on what I said in the Rose Garden: It is absolutely vital that the truth comes out on what happened to Freddie Gray.

And it is my practice not to comment on the legal processes involved; that would not be appropriate. But I can tell you that justice needs to be served. All the evidence needs to be presented. Those individuals who are charged obviously are also entitled to due process and rule of law. And so I want to make sure that our legal system runs the way it should.

And the Justice Department and our new Attorney General is in communications with Baltimore officials to make sure that any assistance we can provide on the investigation is provided. But what I think the people of Baltimore want more than anything else is the truth. That's what people around the country expect. And to the extent that it's appropriate, this administration will help local officials get to the bottom of exactly what happened.

In the meantime, I'm gratified that we've seen the constructive, thoughtful protests that have been taking place, peaceful but clear calls for accountability -- that those have been managed over the last couple of days in a way that's ultimately positive for Baltimore and positive for the country. And I hope that approach to nonviolent protest and community engagement continues.

And finally, as I've said for the last year, we are going to continue to work with the task force that we put together post-Ferguson. I'm actually going to be talking to mayors who are interested in figuring ways to rebuild trust between the community and police, and to focus on some of the issues that were raised by the task force right after this meeting. Our efforts to make sure that we're providing greater opportunity for young people in these communities -- all those things are going to be continuing top priorities for the administration. And we'll probably have some more announcements and news about that in the days and weeks to come.

All right. Thank you very much, everybody.

1. According to President Barack Obama, what is the significance of World Press Freedom Day?

"HOW WOODROW WILSON'S PROPAGANDA MACHINE CHANGED AMERICAN JOURALISM," BY CHRISTOPHER B. DALY, FROM *THE CONVERSATION*, APRIL 27, 2017

When the United States declared war on Germany 100 years ago, the impact on the news business was swift and dramatic.

In its crusade to "make the world safe for democracy," the Wilson administration took immediate steps at home to curtail one of the pillars of democracy – press freedom – by implementing a plan to control, manipulate and censor all news coverage, on a scale never seen in U.S. history.

Following the lead of the Germans and British, Wilson elevated propaganda and censorship to strategic elements of all-out war. Even before the U.S. entered the war, Wilson had expressed the expectation that his fellow Americans would show what he considered "loyalty."

Immediately upon entering the war, the Wilson administration brought the most modern management techniques to bear in the area of government-press relations. Wilson started one of the earliest uses of government propaganda. He waged a campaign of intimidation and outright suppression against those ethnic and socialist papers that continued to oppose the war.

Taken together, these wartime measures added up to an unprecedented assault on press freedom.

I study the history of American journalism, but before I started researching this episode, I had thought that the government's efforts to control the press began with President Roosevelt during WWII. What I discovered is that Wilson was the pioneer of a system that persists to this day.

All Americans have a stake in getting the truth in wartime. A warning from the WWI era, widely attributed to Sen. Hiram Johnson, puts the issue starkly: "The first casualty when war comes is truth."

MOBILIZING FOR WAR

Within a week of Congress declaring war, on April 13, 1917, Wilson issued an executive order creating a new federal agency that would put the government in the business of actively shaping press coverage.

That agency was the Committee on Public Information, which would take on the task of explaining to millions of young men being drafted into military service – and to the millions of other Americans who had so recently supported neutrality – why they should now support war.

The new agency – which journalist Stephen Ponder called "the nation's first ministry of information" – was usually referred to as the Creel Committee for its chairman, George Creel, who had been a journalist before the war. From the start, the CPI was "a veritable magnet" for political progressives of all stripes – intellectuals, muckrakers, even some socialists – all sharing a sense of the threat to democracy posed by German militarism. Idealistic journalists like S.S. McClure and Ida Tarbell signed on, joining others who shared their belief in Wilson's crusade to make the world safe for democracy.

At the time, most Americans got their news through newspapers, which were flourishing in the years just before the rise of radio and the invention of the weekly news magazine. In New York City, according to my research, nearly two dozen papers were published every day – in English alone – while dozens of weeklies served ethnic audiences.

Starting from scratch, Creel organized the CPI into several divisions using the full array of communications.

The Speaking Division recruited 75,000 specialists who became known as "Four-Minute Men" for their ability to lay out Wilson's war aims in short speeches.

The Film Division produced newsreels intended to rally support by showing images in movie theaters that emphasized the heroism of the Allies and the barbarism of the Germans.

The Foreign Language Newspaper Division kept an eye on the hundreds of weekly and daily U.S. newspapers published in languages other than English.

Another CPI unit secured free advertising space in American publications to promote campaigns aimed at selling war bonds, recruiting new soldiers, stimulating patriotism and reinforcing the message that the nation was involved in a great crusade against a bloodthirsty, antidemocratic enemy.

Some of the advertising showed off the work of another CPI unit. The Division of Pictorial Publicity was led by a group of volunteer artists and illustrators. Their output included some of the most enduring images of this period, including the portrait by James Montgomery Flagg of a vigorous Uncle Sam, declaring, "I WANT YOU FOR THE U.S. ARMY!"

Other ads showed cruel "Huns" with blood dripping from their pointed teeth, hinting that Germans were guilty of bestial attacks on defenseless women and children. "Such a civilization is not fit to live," one ad concluded.

Creel denied that his committee's work amounted to propaganda, but he acknowledged that he was engaged in a battle of perceptions. "The war was not fought in France alone," he wrote in 1920, after it was all over, describing the

CPI as "a plain publicity proposition, a vast enterprise in salesmanship, the world's greatest adventure in advertising."

BURIED IN PAPER

For most journalists, the bulk of their contact with the CPI was through its News Division, which became a veritable engine of propaganda on a par with similar government operations in Germany and England but of a sort previously unknown in the United States.

In the brief year and a half of its existence, the CPI's News Division set out to shape the coverage of the war in U.S. newspapers and magazines. One technique was to bury journalists in paper, creating and distributing some 6,000 press releases – or, on average, handing out more than 10 a day.

The whole operation took advantage of a fact of journalistic life. In times of war, readers hunger for news and newspapers attempt to meet that demand. But at the same time, the government was taking other steps to restrict reporters' access to soldiers, generals, munitions-makers and others involved in the struggle. So, after stimulating the demand for news while artificially restraining the supply, the government stepped into the resulting vacuum and provided a vast number of official stories that looked like news.

Most editors found the supply irresistible. These government-written offerings appeared in at least 20,000 newspaper columns each week, by one estimate, at a cost to taxpayers of only US$76,000.

In addition, the CPI issued a set of voluntary "guidelines" for U.S. newspapers, to help those patriotic editors who wanted to support the war effort (with the implication that those editors who did not follow the guidelines were less patriotic than those who did).

The CPI News Division then went a step further, creating something new in the American experience: a daily newspaper published by the government itself. Unlike the "partisan press" of the 19th century, the Wilson-era Official Bulletin was entirely a governmental publication, sent out each day and posted in every military installation and post office as well as in many other government offices. In some respects, it is the closest the United States has come to a paper like the Soviet Union's *Pravda* or China's *People's Daily*.

The CPI was, in short, a vast effort in propaganda. The committee built upon the pioneering efforts of public relations man Ivy Lee and others, developing the young field of public relations to new heights. The CPI hired a sizable fraction of all the Americans who had any experience in this new field, and it trained many more.

One of the young recruits was Edward L. Bernays, a nephew of Sigmund Freud and a pioneer in theorizing about human thoughts and emotions. Bernays volunteered for the CPI and threw himself into the work. His outlook – a mixture of idealism about the cause of spreading democracy and cynicism about the methods involved – was typical of many at the agency.

"The conscious and intelligent manipulation of the organized habits and opinions of the masses is an important element in democratic society," Bernays wrote a few years after the war. "Propaganda is the executive arm of the invisible government."

All in all, the CPI proved quite effective in using advertising and PR to instill nationalistic feelings in Americans. Indeed, many veterans of the CPI's campaign of persuasion went into careers in advertising during the 1920s.

The full bundle of techniques pioneered by Wilson during the Great War were updated and used by later presidents when they sent U.S. forces into battle. Now, as the Trump administration begins to engage in military operations abroad, the American experience in WWI provides some timely warnings: The news media and all U.S. citizens should demand not propaganda, but accurate information in times of hostilities, and the government should never be allowed to equate dissent with disloyalty.

1. How did the US use propaganda in World War I? What made this use different from propaganda in the past?

2. According to the author, what long-term impact did this have on the press?

EXCERPT FROM "S. RES. 150 - A RESOLUTION RECOGNIZING THREATS TO FREEDOM OF THE PRESS AND EXPRESSION AROUND THE WORLD AND REAFFIRMING FREEDOM OF THE PRESS AS A PRIORITY IN EFFORTS OF THE UNITED STATES GOVERNMENT TO PROMOTE DEMOCRACY AND GOOD GOVERNANCE," FROM THE UNITED STATES CONGRESS, MAY 3 2017

Recognizing threats to freedom of the press and expression around the world and reaffirming freedom of the press as a priority in efforts of the United States Government to promote democracy and good governance.

RESOLUTION

Recognizing threats to freedom of the press and expression around the world and reaffirming freedom of the press as a priority in efforts of the United States Government to promote democracy and good governance.

Whereas Article 19 of the United Nations Universal Declaration of Human Rights, adopted in Paris, France, on December 10, 1948, states, "Everyone has the right to freedom of opinion and expression; this right includes freedom to hold opinions without interference and to seek, receive and impart information and ideas through any media and regardless of frontiers.";

Whereas, in 1993, the United Nations General Assembly proclaimed May 3 of each year as "World Press Freedom Day" to celebrate the fundamental principles of freedom of the press, evaluate freedom of the press around the world, defend against attacks on the independence of the media, and pay tribute to journalists who have lost their lives in the exercise of their profession;

Whereas, on December 18, 2013, the United Nations General Assembly adopted a resolution (United Nations General Assembly Resolution 163 (2013)) on the safety of journalists and the issue of impunity, that unequivocally condemns, in both conflict and nonconflict situations, all attacks on and violence against journalists and media workers, including torture, extrajudicial killing, enforced disappearance, arbitrary detention, and intimidation and harassment;

Whereas the theme for the 2017 World Press Freedom Day, is "Critical Minds for Critical Times: Media's role in advancing peaceful, just and inclusive societies";

Whereas the Daniel Pearl Freedom of the Press Act of 2009 (22 U.S.C. 2151 note; Public Law 111–166), which was passed by unanimous consent in the Senate and signed into law by President Barack Obama in 2010, expanded the annual Human Rights Reports of the Department of State to include the examination of freedom of the press;

Whereas, the 2016 World Press Freedom Index, published by Reporters Without Borders in April 2016, indicated "a climate of fear and tension combined with increasing control over newsrooms by governments and private sector interests";

Whereas, the 2016 World Press Freedom Index identified a decline in media freedom across all indicators, especially the destruction of media infrastructure, like the facilities and equipment of media, and the adoption of legislative frameworks that unjustly penalize journalists for doing their work;

Whereas, according to the Committee to Protect Journalists, in 2016, the three deadliest countries for journalists were Syria, Yemen, and Iraq, with more than half of the journalists killed in combat or crossfire, for the first time since the Committee to Protect Journalists began keeping records;

Whereas, according to the Committee to Protect Journalists, in 2016, 48 journalists were killed in cases where the motive was confirmed to be related to their reporting, 28 journalists were killed in cases where the motive was unconfirmed, and 2 media workers were killed;

Whereas, according to the Committee to Protect Journalists, impunity for the murder of journalists remains systemic, with the killers going free in 9 out of 10 cases;

Whereas, according to the Committee to Protect Journalists, as of December 1, 2016, 259 journalists worldwide were in prison, the highest number recorded since the group began systematically tracking imprisonment in 1990;

Whereas, according to the Freedom House report "Freedom of the Press 2017", only 13 percent of the world's population enjoys a Free press, meaning "coverage of political news is robust, the safety of journalists is guaranteed, state intrusion in media affairs is minimal, and the press is not subject to onerous legal or economic pressures.";

Whereas freedom of the press is a key component of democratic governance, activism in civil society, and socioeconomic development; and

Whereas freedom of the press enhances public accountability, transparency, and participation: Now, therefore, be it

Resolved, That the Senate—

(1) expresses concern about the threats to freedom of the press and expression around the world;

(2) welcomes the celebration of World Press Freedom Day 2017 on May 3, 2017;

(3) commends journalists and media workers around the world for their essential role in promoting government accountability, defending democratic activity, and strengthening civil society, despite threats to their safety;

(4) pays tribute to journalists who have lost their lives or liberty carrying out their work;

(5) calls on governments abroad to implement United Nations General Assembly Resolution (A/RES/68/163) by thoroughly investigating and seeking to resolve outstanding cases of violence against journalists, including murders and kidnappings, while ensuring the protection of witnesses, and by reporting on the status of investigations;

(6) condemns all actions around the world that suppress freedom of the press;

(7) reaffirms the centrality of freedom of the press to efforts of the United States Government to support democracy, mitigate conflict, and promote good governance domestically and around the world; and

(8) calls on the President and the Secretary of State—

(A) to preserve and build upon United States leadership in freedom of the press, on the basis of First Amendment protections;

(B) to improve the means by which the United States Government rapidly identifies, publicizes, and responds to threats against freedom of the press around the world;

(C) to urge foreign governments to conduct transparent investigations and adjudications of the perpetrators of attacks against journalists; and

(D) to highlight the issue of threats against freedom of the press in the annual Human Rights Reports and year round.

1. How does protecting freedom of the press encourage democracy?

2. How does this bill seek to influence freedom of the press around the world?

"H. RES. 536 - SUPPORTING FREEDOM OF THE PRESS IN LATIN AMERICA AND THE CARIBBEAN AND CONDEMNING VIOLATIONS OF PRESS FREEDOM AND VIOLENCE AGAINST JOURNALISTS, BLOGGERS, AND INDIVIDUALS EXERCISING THEIR RIGHT TO FREEDOM OF SPEECH," FROM THE UNITED STATES CONGRESS, DECEMBER 15, 2015

IN THE HOUSE OF REPRESENTATIVES, U.S.,

December 15, 2015.

Whereas despite the strong tradition of independent and critical media in many countries in Latin America and the Caribbean, journalists in some countries are becoming increasingly vulnerable to violence and government harassment;

Whereas, on July 29, 2015, the Western Hemisphere Subcommittee convened a hearing titled "Threats to Press Freedom in the Americas" and Carlos Lauria, Senior Americas Program Coordinator at the Committee to Protect Journalists stated that "Scores of journalists have been killed and disappeared. Media outlets have been bombed and forced into censorship***. Censorship due to violence in Latin America has reached one of its highest points since most of the region was dominated by military rule more than three decades ago.";

Whereas in 2014, Cuban authorities detained 1,817 members of civil society, 31 of whom were independent journalists;

Whereas in Cuba, independent journalists face sustained harassment, including detention and physical abuse from the Castro regime;

Whereas in Ecuador, in September 2015, the government took steps to close the sole press freedom monitoring organization, Fundamedios, for exceeding its corporate charter, but the government relented in the face of international criticism and potential economic reprisals;

Whereas in the country, forced corrections by the government have become a means of institutional censorship;

Whereas according to the Committee to Protect Journalists, Mexico is one of the most dangerous countries in the world for the press;

Whereas in Mexico, over 50 journalists have been killed or have disappeared since 2007, at least 11 reporters have been killed since 2011, 4 of them in direct reprisal for their work;

Whereas according to the Committee to Protect Journalists, at least four journalists have been killed in Brazil in 2015, many times after being tortured and having their bodies mutilated;

Whereas Evany José Metzker, a political blogger in the state of Minas Gerais who had been investigating a child prostitution ring, was found decapitated outside the town of Padre Paraíso;

Whereas according to the Organization of American States (OAS) 2014 Annual Report of the Inter-American Commission on Human Rights, journalists covering protests in Venezuela were subject to assaults, obstruction, detention, raids, threats, censorship orders, and confiscation or destruction of equipment;

Whereas, on April 21, 2015, a lawsuit within the 29th District Tribunal of the Metropolitan area of Caracas charged the journal El Nacional and its Chief Editor Miguel Henrique Otero for "reproducing false information" and was forced to flee Venezuela;

Whereas the Honduran national human rights commissioner reported that eight journalists and social communicators were killed as of September, compared with three in 2013, and dozens of cases in which journalists reported being victims of threats and persecution;

Whereas according to the OAS 2014 Annual Report of the Inter-American Commission on Human Rights, members of the media and nongovernmental organizations (NGOs) stated the press "self-censored" due to fear of reprisal from organized crime or corrupt government officials;

Whereas in Colombia, there were 98 incidents of violence and harassment against journalists, 30 were physically attacked, and 45 were victims of harassment or intimidation due to their reporting;

Whereas members of illegal armed groups sought to inhibit freedom of expression by intimidating, threatening, kidnapping, and killing journalists;

Whereas national and international NGOs reported that local media representatives regularly practiced self-censorship because of threats of violence from these groups;

Whereas according to the OAS 2014 Annual Report of the Inter-American Commission on Human Rights, throughout 2014, Guatemala presented accounts of cases of harassment and the filing of several criminal complaints against a newspaper that criticized the Administration;

Whereas according to the Department of State's Country Reports on Human Rights Practices for 2014 in Nicaragua, the government continued to use direct and indirect means to pressure and seek to close independent radio stations, allegedly for political reasons;

Whereas according to the Department of State's Country Reports on Human Rights Practices for 2014 in Argentina, a survey released of 830 journalists throughout the country indicated 53 percent of respondents worked for a media outlet that self-censored content; and

Whereas almost half the journalists surveyed said they self-censored in their reporting on the national government: Now, therefore, be it

Resolved, That the House of Representatives—

(1) supports a free press in Latin America and the Caribbean and condemns violations of press freedom and violence against journalists;

(2) urges countries in the region to implement recommendations from the Organization of American States' Office of the Special Rapporteur for Freedom of Expression to its Member States;

(3) urges countries in Latin America and the Caribbean to be vocal in condemning violations of press freedom, violence against journalists, and the culture of impunity that leads to self-censorship;

(4) urges countries in the Western Hemisphere to uphold the principles outlined in the Inter-American Democratic Charter and urges their neighbors in the region to stand by the charter they are a party to; and

(5) urges the United States Agency for International Development and the Department of State to assist, when appropriate, the media in closed societies to promote an open and free press.

1. According to this bill, what issues face freedom of the press in Latin America and the Caribbean?

2. Choose one country above and explain challenges to freedom of the press. How might actions taken by the US help journalists there?

"AS NATIONAL NEWS GROUPS REACT, HOUSE WON'T BACK DOWN OVER PRESS ACCESS," BY KATIE BIERI, FROM *CRONKITE NEWS*, AUGUST 4, 2016

WASHINGTON – As state and national press advocates reacted Friday to what they called "invasive" background checks for media at the Arizona Legislature, House Republicans were refusing to back down on an issue they insist is being blown out of proportion.

"It's not about banning media from the floor," but about the need for increased security in the Capitol, said Stephanie Grisham, a spokeswoman for the Republican Majority Caucus. She said recent news reports that charged reporters had been barred were "completely inaccurate."

The dispute began Monday when House administrators asked nonstaff to submit to a lengthy background form that included Social Security numbers and other personal information, information that was taken off the form later in the week.

But Capitol press refused to comply with the revised form, which House officials are requiring for anyone with access to a nonpublic part of the Capitol. As a result, more than a dozen photographers and reporters were turned away from the House floor Thursday and forced to cover that day's session from the gallery.

National free-speech organizations said Friday they were concerned about the background check, some more than others.

"It's certainly very troubling to hear that reporters would lose that kind of access to lawmakers," said Melissa Yeager, senior staff writer at the Sunlight Foundation in Washington.

Yeager said there have been similar conflicts in the legislatures of Missouri, Kansas and Maine when lawmakers in those states limited the access of reporters.

"There are a lot of relationships that are built by having access to the floor, to be able to talk to lawmakers and see who they're interacting with," Yeager said. "It creates better reporting when people can have a conversation and ask questions. Putting someone up in the balcony, where they don't have that sort of access, will definitely hinder reporting."

Newseum CEO Jeff Herbst agreed that it's in the best interest of the public to have reporters as close to local officials as possible.

"People are hungry to understand what elected representatives are doing and how they're best representing them," Herbst said.

He downplayed the suggestion that there is an increased security risk, noting that the dangers of sitting in a legislature are minimal compared to other occupational hazards.

"It's far more dangerous driving on the road each day, but no one says to ban all drivers," Herbst said.

But Grisham said the security concerns are very real, citing recent protests and activity at the Capitol, including a March 28 incident that led to the arrest of one man.

"These are new times and this is a really heightened political climate," Grisham said.

She emphasized that all non-staff must comply with the new rules, including vendors, interns – even the house chaplain and the doctor of the day. And she said the new rules should not have come as a surprise to anyone.

"This security plan, and the protocols within, have been in the works for a year," Grisham said. "Nothing happened yesterday."

Morgan Loew, president of the Arizona First Amendment Coalition, was taken aback by the requirements, which were put forward by House Speaker David Gowan.

"This does have a chilling effect on the watchdogs of our lawmakers," Loew said. "We certainly, vehemently, disagree with this decision."

Loew said members of his coalition are reviewing the policy and considering next steps, including possible legal action.

"When we are singled out for something that impedes our ability to carry out our rights under the First Amendment, which is freedom of expression, freedom of press, there is a problem," Loew said.

But Ken Paulson, president of the First Amendment Center and former editor of *USA Today*, said that what happened at the Capitol does not necessarily violate the First Amendment.

"Given that reporters are still able to see and hear the proceedings, this isn't a First Amendment issue," Paulson said in an email Friday. "It does make reporters' jobs harder and makes legislators less accessible and accountable to the public and press – which may be what the legislature intended."

Grisham said that there are currently no plans to change this new requirement.

She adamantly denied published reports that Gowan was targeting *Arizona Capitol Times* reporter Hank Stephenson with the new rule. Those same reports said Stephenson has a misdemeanor conviction that could fall under the new rules.

Stephenson wrote a story in January criticizing the speaker's use of state vehicles, leading Gowan to reimburse the state with $12,000 of his own money.

Grisham said House staff had no knowledge Stephenson had a conviction on his record, and said she is on good terms with him.

"He and I get along very, very well," Grisham said.

1. Why is access important to ensuring freedom of the press?

2. What balances might be effective to ensure access while maintaining some privacy?

CHAPTER 3

WHAT THE COURTS SAY

G iven the kinds of issues that journalists often report on, the courts have often heard cases regarding issues of press freedom and the rights of newspapers or other publications to release information. Many of these cases are brought by state or federal governments in instances when publications are seen as threatening national security, a difficult concern to address due to the need for transparency balanced with the safety of the country. As we'll see in these rulings, the courts are not always in agreement on where the line rests between national security and the need for governmental transparency. At the same time, lawsuits can be used to strengthen freedom of the press by revealing ways in which the state tries to restrict journalism.

EXCERPT FROM *NEAR V. STATE OF MINNESOTA EX REL. OLSON*, UNITED STATES SUPREME COURT, JUNE 1, 1931

1. A Minnesota statute declares that one who engages "in the business of regularly and customarily producing, publishing," etc., "a malicious, scandalous and defamatory newspaper, magazine or other periodical," is guilty of a nuisance, and authorizes suits, in the name of the State, in which such periodicals may be abated and their publishers enjoined from future violations. In such a suit, malice may be inferred from the fact of publication. The defendant is permitted to prove, as a defense, that his publications were true and published "with good motives and for justifiable ends." Disobedience of an injunction is punishable as a contempt. Held unconstitutional, as applied to publications charging neglect of duty and corruption upon the part of law-enforcing officers of the State. Pp. 283 U. S. 704, 283 U. S. 709, 283 U. S. 712, 283 U. S. 722.

2. Liberty of the press is within the liberty safeguarded by the due process clause of the Fourteenth Amendment from invasion by state action. P. 283 U. S. 707.

3. Liberty of the press is not an absolute right, and the State may punish its abuse. P. 283 U. S. 708.

4. In passing upon the constitutionality of the statute, the court has regard for substance, and not for form; the statute must be tested by its operation and effect. P. 283 U. S. 708.

5. Cutting through mere details of procedure, the operation and effect of the statute is that public authorities may bring a publisher before a judge upon a charge of conducting a business of publishing scandalous and defamatory matter -- in particular, that the matter consists of charges against public officials of official dereliction -- and, unless the publisher is able and disposed to satisfy the judge that the charges are true and are published with good motives and for justifiable ends, his newspaper or periodical is suppressed and further publication is made punishable as a contempt. This is the essence of censorship. P. 283 U. S. 713.

6. A statute authorizing such proceedings in restraint of publication is inconsistent with the conception of the liberty of the press as historically conceived and guaranteed. P. 283 U. S. 713.

7. The chief purpose of the guaranty is to prevent previous restraints upon publication. The libeler, however, remains criminally and civilly responsible for his libels. P. 283 U. S. 713.

8. There are undoubtedly limitations upon the immunity from previous restraint of the press, but they are not applicable in this case. P. 283 U. S. 715.

9. The liberty of the press has been especially cherished in this country as respects publications censuring public officials and charging official misconduct. P. 283 U. S. 716.

10. Public officers find their remedies for false accusations in actions for redress and punishment under the libel laws, and not in proceedings to restrain the publication of newspapers and periodicals. P. 283 U. S. 718.

11. The fact that the liberty of the press may be abused by miscreant purveyors of scandal does not make any the less necessary the immunity from previous restraint in dealing with official misconduct. P. 283 U. S. 720.

12. Characterizing the publication of charges of official misconduct as a "business," and the business as a nuisance, does not avoid the constitutional guaranty; nor does it matter that the periodical is largely or chiefly devoted to such charges. P. 283 U. S. 720.

13. The guaranty against previous restraint extends to publications charging official derelictions that amount to crimes. P. 283 U. S. 720.

14. Permitting the publisher to show in defense that the matter published is true and is published with good motives and for justifiable ends does not justify the statute. P. 283 U. S. 721.

15. Nor can it be sustained as a measure for preserving the public peace and preventing assaults and crime. Pp. 283 U. S. 721, 283 U. S. 722.

APPEAL from a decree which sustained an injunction abating the publication of a periodical as malicious, scandalous and defamatory, and restraining future publication. The suit was based on a Minnesota statute. See also s.c., 174 Minn. 457, 219 N.W. 770.

MR. CHIEF JUSTICE HUGHES delivered the opinion of the Court.

Chapter 285 of the Session Laws of Minnesota for the year 1925[1] provides for the abatement, as a public nuisance, of a "malicious, scandalous and defamatory newspaper, magazine or other periodical." Section one of the Act is as follows:

"Section 1. Any person who, as an individual, or as a member or employee of a firm, or association or organization, or as an officer, director, member or employee of a corporation, shall be engaged in the business of regularly or customarily producing, publishing or circulating, having in possession, selling or giving away"

"(a) an obscene, lewd and lascivious newspaper, magazine, or other periodical, or"

"(b) a malicious, scandalous and defamatory newspaper, magazine or other periodical,"

is guilty of a nuisance, and all persons guilty of such nuisance may be enjoined, as hereinafter provided.

"Participation in such business shall constitute a commission of such nuisance and render the participant liable and subject to the proceedings, orders and judgments provided for in this Act. Ownership, in whole or in part, directly or indirectly, of any such periodical, or of any stock or interest in any corporation or organization which owns the same in whole or in part, or which publishes the same, shall constitute such participation."

"In actions brought under (b) above, there shall be available the defense that the truth was published with good motives and for justifiable ends and in such actions the plaintiff shall not have the right to report (sic) to issues or editions of periodicals taking place more than three months before the commencement of the action."

Section two provides that, whenever any such nuisance is committed or exists, the County Attorney of any county where any such periodical is published or circulated, or, in case of his failure or refusal to proceed upon written request in good faith of a reputable citizen, the Attorney General, or, upon like failure or refusal of the latter, any citizen of the county may maintain an action in the district court of the county in the name of the State to enjoin perpetually the persons committing or maintaining any such nuisance from further committing or maintaining it. Upon such evidence as the court shall deem sufficient, a temporary injunction may be granted. The defendants have the right to plead by demurrer or answer, and the plaintiff may demur or reply as in other cases.

The action, by section three, is to be " governed by the practice and procedure applicable to civil actions for injunctions," and, after trial, the court may enter judgment permanently enjoining the defendants found guilty of violating the Act from continuing the violation, and, "in and by such judgment, such nuisance may be wholly abated." The court is empowered, as in other cases of contempt, to punish disobedience to a temporary or permanent injunction by fine of not more than $1,000 or by imprisonment in the county jail for not more than twelve months.

Under this statute, clause (b), the County Attorney of Hennepin County brought this action to enjoin the publication of what was described as a " malicious, scandalous and defamatory newspaper, magazine and periodical" known as *"The Saturday Press,"* published by the defendants in the city of Minneapolis. The complaint alleged that the defendants, on September 24, 1927, and on eight subsequent dates in October and November, 1927, published and circulated editions of that periodical which were "largely devoted to malicious, scandalous and defamatory articles" concerning Charles G. Davis, Frank W. Brunskill, the Minneapolis Tribune, the Minneapolis Journal, Melvin C. Passolt, George E. Leach, the Jewish Race, the members of the Grand Jury of Hennepin County impaneled in November, 1927, and then holding office, and other persons, as more fully appeared in exhibits annexed to the complaint, consisting of copies of the articles described and constituting 327 pages of the record. While the complaint did not so allege, it appears from the briefs of both parties that Charles G. Davis was a special law enforcement officer employed by a civic organization, that George E. Leach was Mayor of Minneapolis, that Frank W. Brunskill was its Chief of Police, and that Floyd B. Olson (the relator in this action) was County Attorney.

Without attempting to summarize the contents of the voluminous exhibits attached to the complaint, we deem it sufficient to say that the articles charged in substance that a Jewish gangster was in control of gambling, bootlegging and racketeering in Minneapolis, and that law enforcing officers and agencies were not energetically performing their duties. Most of the charges were directed against the Chief of Police; he was charged with gross neglect of duty, illicit relations with gangsters, and with participation in graft. The County Attorney was charged with knowing the existing conditions and with failure to take adequate measures to remedy them. The Mayor was accused of inefficiency and dereliction. One member of the grand jury was stated to be in sympathy with the gangsters. A special grand jury and a special prosecutor were demanded to deal with the situation in general, and, in particular, to investigate an attempt to assassinate one Guilford, one of the original defendants, who, it appears from the articles, was shot by gangsters after the first issue of the periodical had been published. There is no question but that the articles made serious accusations against the public officers named and others in connection with the prevalence of crimes and the failure to expose and punish them.

At the beginning of the action, on November 22, 1927, and upon the verified complaint, an order was made directing the defendants to show cause why a temporary injunction should not issue and meanwhile forbidding the defendants to publish, circulate or have in their possession any editions of the periodical from September 24, 1927, to November 19, 1927, inclusive, and from publishing, circulating, or having in their possession, "any future editions of said *The Saturday Press*" and "any publication, known by any other name whatsoever containing malicious, scandalous and defamatory matter of the kind alleged in plaintiff's complaint herein or otherwise."

The defendants demurred to the complaint upon the ground that it did not state facts sufficient to constitute a cause of action, and on this demurrer challenged the constitutionality of the statute. The District Court overruled the demurrer and certified the question of constitutionality to the

Supreme Court of the State. The Supreme Court sustained the statute (174 Minn. 457, 219 N.W. 770), and it is conceded by the appellee that the Act was thus held to be valid over the objection that it violated not only the state constitution, but also the Fourteenth Amendment of the Constitution of the United States.

Thereupon, the defendant Near, the present appellant, answered the complaint. He averred that he was the sole owner and proprietor of the publication in question. He admitted the publication of the articles in the issues described in the complaint, but denied that they were malicious, scandalous or defamatory as alleged. He expressly invoked the protection of the due process clause of the Fourteenth Amendment. The case then came on for trial. The plaintiff offered in evidence the verified complaint, together with the issues of the publication in question, which were attached to the complaint as exhibits. The defendant objected to the introduction of the evidence, invoking the constitutional provisions to which his answer referred. The objection was overruled, no further evidence was presented, and the plaintiff rested. The defendant then rested without offering evidence. The plaintiff moved that the court direct the issue of a permanent injunction, and this was done.

The District Court made findings of fact which followed the allegations of the complaint and found in general terms that the editions in question were "chiefly devoted to malicious, scandalous and defamatory articles" concerning the individuals named. The court further found that the defendants, through these publications,

"did engage in the business of regularly and customarily producing, publishing and circulating a malicious, scandalous and defamatory newspaper," and that "the said publication" "under said name of *The Saturday Press*, or any other name, constitutes a public nuisance under the laws of the State." Judgment was thereupon entered adjudging that "the newspaper, magazine and periodical known as The Saturday Press," as a public nuisance, "be and is hereby abated." The Judgment perpetually enjoined the defendants

> "from producing, editing, publishing, circulating, having in their possession, selling or giving away any publication whatsoever which is a malicious, scandalous or defamatory newspaper, as defined by law," and also "from further conducting said nuisance under the name and title of said The *Saturday Press* or any other name or title."

The defendant Near appealed from this judgment to the Supreme Court of the State, again asserting his right under the Federal Constitution, and the judgment was affirmed upon the authority of the former decision. With respect to the contention that the judgment went too far, and prevented the defendants from publishing any kind of a newspaper, the court observed that the assignments of error did not go to the form of the judgment, and that the lower court had not been asked to modify it. The court added that it saw no reason

> "for defendants to construe the judgment as restraining them from operating a newspaper in harmony with the public welfare, to which all must yield,"

that the allegations of the complaint had beenfound to be true, and, though this was an equitable action, defendants had not indicated a desire "to conduct their business in the usual and legitimate manner."

From the judgment as thus affirmed, the defendant Near appeals to this Court.

This statute, for the suppression as a public nuisance of a newspaper or periodical, is unusual, if not unique, and raises questions of grave importance transcending the local interests involved in the particular action. It is no longer open to doubt that the liberty of the press, and of speech, is within the liberty safeguarded by the due process clause of the Fourteenth Amendment from invasion by state action. It was found impossible to conclude that this essential personal liberty of the citizen was left unprotected by the general guaranty of fundamental rights of person and property. *Gitlow v. New York*, 268 U. S. 652, 268 U. S. 666; *Whitney v. California*,274 U. S. 357, 274 U. S. 362, 274 U. S. 373; *Fiske v. Kansas*, 274 U. S. 380, 274 U. S. 382; *Stromberg v. California, ante*, p. 283 U. S. 359. In maintaining this guaranty, the authority of the State to enact laws to promote the health, safety, morals and general welfare of its people is necessarily admitted. The limits of this sovereign power must always be determined with appropriate regard to the particular subject of its exercise. Thus, while recognizing the broad discretion of the legislature in fixing rates to be charged by those undertaking a public service, this Court has decided that the owner cannot constitutionally be deprived of his right to a fair return, because that is deemed to be of the essence of ownership. *Railroad Commission Cases*, 116 U. S. 307, 116 U. S. 331; *Northern Pacific Ry. Co. v. North Dakota*, 236 U. S. 585,236 U. S. 596. So, while liberty of contract is not an absolute right, and the wide field of activity in the making of contracts is subject to legislative supervision (*Frisbie v.*

United States, 157 U. S. 161, 157 U. S. 165), this Court has held that the power of the State stops short of interference with what are deemed to be certain indispensable requirements of the liberty assured, notably with respect to the fixing of prices and wages. *Tyson Bros. v. Banton*, 273 U. S. 418; *Ribnik v. McBride*, 277 U. S. 350; *Adkins v. Children's Hospital*, 261 U. S. 525, 261 U. S. 560, 261 U. S. 561. Liberty of speech, and of the press, is also not an absolute right, and the State may punish its abuse. *Whitney v. California, supra*; *Stromberg v. California, supra*. Liberty, in each of its phases, has its history and connotation, and, in the present instance, the inquiry is as to the historic conception of the liberty of the press and whether the statute under review violates the essential attributes of that liberty.

The appellee insists that the questions of the application of the statute to appellant's periodical, and of the construction of the judgment of the trial court, are not presented for review; that appellant's sole attack was upon the constitutionality of the statute, however it might be applied. The appellee contends that no question either of motive in the publication, or whether the decree goes beyond the direction of the statute, is before us. The appellant replies that, in his view, the plain terms of the statute were not departed from in this case, and that, even if they were, the statute is nevertheless unconstitutional under any reasonable construction of its terms. The appellant states that he has not argued that the temporary and permanent injunctions were broader than were warranted by the statute; he insists that what was done was properly done if the statute is valid, and that the action taken under the statute is a fair indication of its scope.

With respect to these contentions, it is enough to say that, in passing upon constitutional questions, the court has regard to substance, and not to mere matters of form, and that, in accordance with familiar principles, the statute must be tested by its operation and effect. *Henderson v. Mayor*, 92 U. S. 259,92 U. S. 268; *Bailey v. Alabama*, 219 U.S. 219, 219 U. S. 244; *United States v. Reynolds*, 235 U. S. 133, 235 U. S. 148,235 U. S. 149; *St. Louis Southwestern R. Co. v. Arkansas*, 235 U. S. 350, 235 U. S. 362; *Mountain Timber Co. v. Washington*, 243 U. S. 219, 243 U. S. 237. That operation and effect we think is clearly shown by the record in this case. We are not concerned with mere errors of the trial court, if there be such, in going beyond the direction of the statute as construed by the Supreme Court of the State. It is thus important to note precisely the purpose and effect of the statute as the state court has construed it.

First. The statute is not aimed at the redress of individual or private wrongs. Remedies for libel remain available and unaffected. The statute, said the state court, "is not directed at threatened libel, but at an existing business which, generally speaking, involves more than libel." It is aimed at the distribution of scandalous matter as "detrimental to public morals and to the general welfare," tending "to disturb the peace of the community" and "to provoke assaults and the commission of crime." In order to obtain an injunction to suppress the future publication of the newspaper or periodical, it is not necessary to prove the falsity of the charges that have been made in the publication condemned. In the present action, there was no allegation that the matter published was not true. It is alleged, and the statute requires the allegation, that the publication was "malicious." But, as in prosecutions for libel, there is no requirement of proof by the State of malice in fact, as distinguished from malice inferred from the mere publication of the defamatory matter.[2] The judgment in this case proceeded upon the mere proof of publication. The statute permits the defense not of the truth alone, but only that the truth was published with good motives and for justifiable ends. It is apparent that, under the statute, the publication is to be regarded as defamatory if it injures reputation, and that it is scandalous if it circulates charges of reprehensible conduct, whether criminal or otherwise, and the publication is thus deemed to invite public reprobation and to constitute a public scandal. The court sharply defined the purpose of the statute, bringing out the precise point, in these words:

> "There is no constitutional right to publish a fact merely because it is true. It is a matter of common knowledge that prosecutions under the criminal libel statutes do not result in efficient repression or suppression of the evils of scandal. Men who are the victims of such assaults seldom resort to the courts. This is especially true if their sins are exposed and the only question relates to whether it was done with good motives and for justifiable ends. This law is not for the protection of the person attacked, nor to punish the wrongdoer. It is for the protection of the pubic welfare."

Second. The statute is directed not simply at the circulation of scandalous and defamatory statements with regard to private citizens, but at the continued publication by newspapers and periodicals of charges against public officers of corruption, malfeasance in office, or serious neglect of duty. Such charges, by their very nature, create a public scandal. They are scandalous and defamatory within the meaning of the statute, which has its normal operation in relation to publications dealing prominently and chiefly with the alleged derelictions of public officers.[3]

Third. The object of the statute is not punishment, in the ordinary sense, but suppression of the offending newspaper or periodical. The reason for the enactment, as the state court has said, is that prosecutions to enforce penal statutes for libel do not result in "efficient repression or suppression of the evils of scandal." Describing the business of publication as a public nuisance does not obscure the substance of the proceeding which the statute authorizes. It is the continued publication of scandalous and defamatory matter that constitutes the business and the declared nuisance. In the case of public officers, it is the reiteration of charges of official misconduct, and the fact that the newspaper or periodical is principally devoted to that purpose, that exposes it to suppression. In the present instance, the proof was that nine editions of the newspaper or periodical in question were published on successive dates, and that they were chiefly devoted to charges against public officers and in relation to the prevalence and protection of crime. In such a case, these officers are not left to their ordinary remedy in a suit for libel, or the authorities to a prosecution for criminal libel. Under this statute, a publisher of a newspaper or periodical, undertaking to conduct a campaign to expose and to censure official derelictions, and devoting his publication principally to that purpose, must face not simply the possibility of a verdict against him in a suit or prosecution for libel, but a determination that his newspaper or periodical is a public nuisance to be abated, and that this abatement and suppression will follow unless he is prepared with legal evidence to prove the truth of the charges and also to satisfy the court that, in addition to being true, the matter was published with good motives and for justifiable ends.

This suppression is accomplished by enjoining publication, and that restraint is the object and effect of the statute.

Fourth. The statute not only operates to suppress the offending newspaper or periodical, but to put the publisher under an effective censorship. When a newspaper or periodical is found to be "malicious, scandalous, and defamatory," and is suppressed as such, resumption of publication is punishable as a contempt of court by fine or imprisonment. Thus, where a newspaper or periodical has been suppressed because of the circulation of charges against public officers of official misconduct, it would seem to be clear that the renewal of the publication of such charges would constitute a contempt, and that the judgment would lay a permanent restraint upon the publisher, to escape which he must satisfy the court as to the character of a new publication. Whether he would be permitted again to publish matter deemed to be derogatory to the same or other public officers would depend upon the court's ruling. In the present instance, the judgment restrained the defendants from

> "publishing, circulating, having in their possession, selling or giving away any publication whatsoever which is a malicious, scandalous or defamatory newspaper, as defined by law."

The law gives no definition except that covered by the words "scandalous and defamatory," and publications charging official misconduct are of that class. While the court, answering the objection that the judgment was too broad, saw no reason for construing it as restraining the defendants "from operating a newspaper in harmony with the public welfare to which all must yield," and said that the defendants had not indicated "any desire to conduct their business in the usual and legitimate manner," the manifest inference is that, at least with respect to a new publication directed against official misconduct, the defendant would be held, under penalty of punishment for contempt as provided in the statute, to a manner of publication which the court considered to be "usual and legitimate" and consistent with the public welfare.

If we cut through mere details of procedure, the operation and effect of the statute, in substance, is that public authorities may bring the owner or publisher of a newspaper or periodical before a judge upon a charge of conducting a business of publishing scandalous and defamatory matter -- in particular, that the matter consists of charges against public officers of official dereliction -- and, unless the owner or publisher is able and disposed to bring competent evidence to satisfy the judge that the charges are true and are published with good motives and for justifiable ends, his newspaper or periodical is suppressed and further publication is made punishable as a contempt. This is of the essence of censorship.

The question is whether a statute authorizing such proceedings in restraint of publication is consistent with the conception of the liberty of the press as historically conceived and guaranteed. In determining the extent of the constitutional protection, it has been generally, if not universally, considered that it is the chief purpose of the guaranty to prevent previous restraints upon publication. The struggle in England, directed against the legislative power of the licenser, resulted in renunciation of the censorship of the press.[4] The liberty deemed to be established was thus described by Blackstone:

> "The liberty of the press is indeed essential to the nature of a free state; but this consists in laying no previous restraints upon publications, and not in freedom from censure for criminal matter when published. Every freeman has an undoubted right to lay what sentiments he pleases before the public; to forbid this is to destroy the freedom of the press; but if he publishes what is improper, mischievous or illegal, he must take the consequence of his own temerity."

The distinction was early pointed out between the extent of the freedom with respect to censorship under our constitutional system and that enjoyed in England. Here, as Madison said,

"the great and essential rights of the people are secured against legislative as well as against executive ambition. They are secured not by laws paramount to prerogative, but by constitutions paramount to laws. This security of the freedom of the press requires that it should be exempt not only from previous restraint by the Executive, a in Great Britain, but from legislative restraint also."

This Court said, in *Patterson v. Colorado*, 205 U. S. 454, 205 U. S. 462:

> "In the first place, the main purpose of such constitutional provisions is 'to prevent all such previous restraints upon publications as had been practiced

by other governments,' and they do not prevent the subsequent punishment of such as may be deemed contrary to the public welfare. The preliminary freedom extends as well to the false as to the true; the subsequent punishment may extend as well to the true as to the false. This was the law of criminal libel apart from statute in most cases, if not in all."

The criticism upon Blackstone's statement has not been because immunity from previous restraint upon publication has not been regarded as deserving of special emphasis, but chiefly because that immunity cannot be deemed to exhaust the conception of the liberty guaranteed by state and federal constitutions. The point of criticism has been "that the mere exemption from previous restraints cannot be all that is secured by the constitutional provisions", and that

"the liberty of the press might be rendered a mockery and a delusion, and the phrase itself a byword, if, while every man was at liberty to publish what he pleased, the public authorities might nevertheless punish him for harmless publications."

But it is recognized that punishment for the abuse of the liberty accorded to the press is essential to the protection of the public, and that the common law rules that subject the libeler to responsibility for the public offense, as well as for the private injury, are not abolished by the protection extended in our constitutions. *Id.*, pp. 883, 884. The law of criminal libel rests upon that secure foundation. There is also the conceded authority of courts to punish for contempt when publications directly tend to prevent the proper discharge of judicial functions. In the present case, we have no occasion to inquire as to the permissible scope of subsequent punishment. For whatever wrong the appellant has committed or may commit by his publications the State appropriately affords both public and private redress by its libel laws. As has been noted, the statute in question does not deal with punishments; it provides for no punishment, except in case of contempt for violation of the court's order, but for suppression and injunction, that is, for restraint upon publication.

The objection has also been made that the principle as to immunity from previous restraint is stated too broadly, if every such restraint is deemed to be prohibited. That is undoubtedly true; the protection even as to previous restraint is not absolutely unlimited. But the limitation has been recognized only in exceptional cases:

> "When a nation is at war, many things that might be said in time of peace are such a hindrance to its effort that their utterance will not be endured so long as men fight, and that no Court could regard them as protected by any constitutional right."

No one would question but that a government might prevent actual obstruction to its recruiting service or the publication of the sailing dates of transports or the number and location of troops.[6] On similar grounds, the primary requirements of decency may be enforced against obscene publications. The security of the community life may be protected against incitements to acts of violence and the overthrow by force of orderly government. The constitutional guaranty of free speech does not

> "protect a man from an injunction against uttering words that may have all the effect of force. *Gompers v. Buck Stove & Range Co.*, 221 U. S. 418, 221 U. S. 439."

These limitations are not applicable here. Nor are we now concerned with questions as to the extent of authority to prevent publications in order to protect private rights according to the principles governing the exercise of the jurisdiction of courts of equity.[7]

The exceptional nature of its limitations places in a strong light the general conception that liberty of the press, historically considered and taken up by the Federal Constitution, has meant, principally, although not exclusively, immunity from previous restraints or censorship. The conception of the liberty of the press in this country had broadened with the exigencies of the colonial period and with the efforts to secure freedom from oppressive administration.[8] That liberty was especially cherished for the immunity it afforded from previous restraint of the publication of censure of public officers and charges of official misconduct. As was said by Chief Justice Parker, in *Commonwealth v. Blanding*, 3 Pick. 304, 313, with respect to the constitution of Massachusetts:

> "Besides, it is well understood, and received as a commentary on this provision for the liberty of the press, that it was intended to prevent all such previous restraints upon publications as had been practiced by other governments, and in early times here, to stifle the efforts of patriots towards enlightening their fellow subjects upon their rights and the duties of rulers. The liberty of the press was to be unrestrained, but he who used it was to be responsible in case of its abuse."

In the letter sent by the Continental Congress (October 26, 1774) to the Inhabitants of Quebec, referring to the "five great rights," it was said:[9]

"The last right we shall mention regards the freedom of the press. The importance of this consists, besides the advancement of truth, science, morality, and arts in general, in its diffusion of liberal sentiments on the administration of Government, its ready communication of thoughts between subjects, and its consequential promotion of union among them whereby oppressive officers are shamed or intimidated into more honourable and just modes of conducting affairs."

Madison, who was the leading spirit in the preparation of the First Amendment of the Federal Constitution, thus described the practice and sentiment which led to the guaranties of liberty of the press in state constitutions:[10]

"In every State, probably, in the Union, the press has exerted a freedom in canvassing the merits and measures of public men of every description which has not been confined to the strict limits of the common law. On this footing the freedom of the press has stood; on this footing it yet stands.... Some degree of abuse is inseparable from the proper use of everything, and in no instance is this more true than in that of the press. It has accordingly been decided by the practice of the States that it is better to leave a few of its noxious branches to their luxuriant growth than, by pruning them away, to injure the vigour of those yielding the proper fruits. And can the wisdom of this policy be doubted by any who reflect that to the press alone, chequered as it is with abuses, the world is indebted for all the triumphs which have been gained by reason and humanity over error and oppression; who reflect that to the same beneficent source the United States owe much of the lights which conducted them to the ranks of a free and independent nation, and which have improved their political system into a shape so auspicious to their happiness? Had 'Sedition Acts,' forbidding every publication that might bring the constituted agents into contempt or disrepute, or that might excite the hatred of the people against the authors of unjust or pernicious measures, been uniformly enforced against the press, might not the United States have been languishing at this day under the infirmities of a sickly Confederation? Might they not, possibly, be miserable colonies, groaning under a foreign yoke?"

The fact that, for approximately one hundred and fifty years, there has been almost an entire absence of attempts to impose previous restraints upon publications relating to the malfeasance of public officers is significant of the deep-seated conviction that such restraints would violate constitutional right. Public officers, whose character and conduct remain open to debate and free discussion in the press, find their remedies for false accusations in actions under libel laws providing for redress and punishment, and not in proceedings to restrain the publication of newspapers and periodicals. The general principle that the constitutional guaranty of the liberty of the press gives immunity from previous restraints has been approved in many decisions under the provisions of state constitutions.[11]

The importance of this immunity has not lessened. While reckless assaults upon public men, and efforts to bring obloquy upon those who are endeavoring faithfully to discharge official duties, exert a baleful influence and deserve the severest condemnation in public opinion, it cannot be said that this abuse is greater, and it is believed to be less, than that which characterized the period in which our institutions took shape. Meanwhile, the administration of government has become more complex, the opportunities for malfeasance and corruption have multiplied, crime has grown to most serious proportions, and the danger of its protection by unfaithful officials and of the impairment of the fundamental security of life and property by criminal alliances and official neglect, emphasizes the primary need of a vigilant and courageous press, especially in great cities. The fact that the liberty of the press may be abused by miscreant purveyors of scandal does not make any the less necessary the immunity of the press from previous restraint in dealing with official misconduct. Subsequent punishment for such abuses as may exist is the appropriate remedy consistent with constitutional privilege.

In attempted justification of the statute, it is said that it deals not with publication per se, but with the "business" of publishing defamation. If, however, the publisher has a constitutional right to publish, without previous restraint, an edition of his newspaper charging official derelictions, it cannot be denied that he may publish subsequent editions for the same purpose. He does not lose his right by exercising it. If his right exists, it may be exercised in publishing nine editions, as in this case, as well as in one edition. If previous restraint is permissible, it may be imposed at once; indeed, the wrong may be as serious in one publication as in several. Characterizing the publication as a business, and the business as a nuisance, does not permit an invasion of the constitutional immunity against restraint. Similarly, it does not matter that the newspaper or periodical is found to be "largely" or "chiefly" devoted to the publication of such derelictions. If the publisher has a right, without previous restraint, to publish them, his right cannot be deemed to be dependent upon his publishing something else, more or less, with the matter to which objection is made.

Nor can it be said that the constitutional freedom from previous restraint is lost because charges are made of derelictions which constitute crimes. With the multiplying provisions of penal codes, and of municipal charters and ordinances carrying penal sanctions, the conduct of public officers is very largely within the purview of criminal statutes. The freedom of the press from previous restraint has never been regarded as limited to such animadversions as lay outside the range of penal enactments. Historically, there is no such limitation; it is inconsistent with the reason which underlies the privilege, as the privilege so limited would be of slight value for the purposes for which it came to be established.

The statute in question cannot be justified by reason of the fact that the publisher is permitted to show, before injunction issues, that the matter published is true and is published with good motives and for justifiable ends. If such a statute, authorizing suppression and injunction on such a basis, is constitutionally valid, it would be equally permissible for the legislature to provide that at any time the publisher of any newspaper could be brought before a court, or even an administrative officer (as the constitutional protection may not be regarded as resting on mere procedural details) and required to produce proof of the truth of his publication, or of what he intended to publish, and of his motives, or stand enjoined. If this can be done, the legislature may provide machinery for determining in the complete exercise of its discretion what are justifiable ends, and restrain publication accordingly. And it would be but a step to a complete system of censorship. The recognition of authority to impose previous restraint upon publication in order to protect the community against the circulation of charges of misconduct, and especially of official misconduct, necessarily would carry with it the admission of the authority of the censor against which the constitutional barrier was erected. The preliminary freedom, by virtue of the very reason for its existence, does not depend, as this Court has said, on proof of truth. *Patterson v. Colorado, supra.*

Equally unavailing is the insistence that the statute is designed to prevent the circulation of scandal which tends to disturb the public peace and to provoke assaults and the commission of crime. Charges of reprehensible conduct, and in particular of official malfeasance, unquestionably create a public scandal, but the theory of the constitutional guaranty is that even a more serious public evil would be caused by authority to prevent publication.

> "To prohibit the intent to excite those unfavorable sentiments against those who administer the Government is equivalent to a prohibition of the actual excitement of them, and to prohibit the actual excitement of them is equivalent to a prohibition of discussions having that tendency and effect, which, again, is equivalent to a protection of those who administer the Government, if they should at any time deserve the contempt or hatred of the people, against being exposed to it by free animadversions on their characters and conduct.[12]"

There is nothing new in the fact that charges of reprehensible conduct may create resentment and the disposition to resort to violent means of redress, but this well understood tendency did not alter the determination to protect the press against censorship and restraint upon publication. As was said in *New Yorker Staats-Zeitung v. Nolan*, 89 N.J. Eq. 387, 388, 105 Atl. 72:

> "If the township may prevent the circulation of a newspaper for no reason other than that some of its inhabitants may violently disagree with it, and resent its circulation by resorting to physical violence, there is no limit to what may be prohibited."

The danger of violent reactions becomes greater with effective organization of defiant groups resenting exposure, and if this consideration warranted legislative interference with the initial freedom of publication, the constitutional protection would be reduced to a mere form of words.

For these reasons we hold the statute, so far as it authorized the proceedings in this action under clause (b) of section one, to be an infringement of the liberty of the press guaranteed by the Fourteenth Amendment. We should add that this decision rests upon the operation and effect of the statute, without regard to the question of the truth of the charges contained in the particular periodical. The fact that the public officers named in this case, and those associated with the charges of official dereliction, may be deemed to be impeccable cannot affect the conclusion that the statute imposes an unconstitutional restraint upon publication.

Judgment reversed.

1. Consider this quote: "There is no constitutional right to publish a fact merely because it is true." What does this mean for freedom of the press, according to this ruling?

2. Why does the court conclude that the judgment should be reversed? What constitutional precedents does their argument rest on?

NEW YORK TIMES CO. V. UNITED STATES, UNITED STATES SUPREME COURT, JUNE 30, 1971

The United States, which brought these actions to enjoin publication in the *New York Times* and in the *Washington Post* of certain classified material, has not met the "heavy burden of showing justification for the enforcement of such a [prior] restraint."

No. 1873, 44 F.2d 544, reversed and remanded; No. 1885, ___ U.S.App.D.C. ___, 446 F.2d 1327, affirmed.

PER CURIAM

We granted certiorari in these cases in which the United States seeks to enjoin the *New York Times* and the *Washington Post* from publishing the contents of a classified study entitled "History of U.S. Decision-Making Process on Viet Nam Policy." *Post*, pp. 942, 943.

"Any system of prior restraints of expression comes to this Court bearing a heavy presumption against its constitutional validity." *Bantam Books, Inc. v. Sullivan*, 372 U. S. 58, 372 U. S. 70 (1963); see also *Near v. Minnesota*, 283 U. S. 697 (1931). The Government "thus carries a heavy burden of showing justification for the imposition of such a restraint." *Organization for a Better Austin v. Keefe*, 402 U. S. 415, 402 U. S. 419 (1971). The District Court for the Southern District of New York, in the *New York Times* case, and the District Court for the District of Columbia and the Court of Appeals for the District of Columbia Circuit, in the *Washington Post* case, held that the Government had not met that burden. We agree.

The judgment of the Court of Appeals for the District of Columbia Circuit is therefore affirmed. The order of the Court of Appeals for the Second Circuit is reversed, and the case is remanded with directions to enter a judgment affirming the judgment of the District Court for the Southern District of New York. The stays entered June 25, 1971, by the Court are vacated. The judgments shall issue forthwith.

So ordered.

* Together with No. 1885, *United States v. Washington Post Co. et al.*, on certiorari to the United States Court of Appeals for the District of Columbia Circuit.

MR. JUSTICE BLACK, with whom MR. JUSTICE DOUGLAS joins, concurring.

I adhere to the view that the Government's case against the *Washington Post* should have been dismissed, and that the injunction against the *New York Times* should have been vacated without oral argument when the cases were first presented to this Court. I believe that every moment's continuance of the injunctions against these newspapers amounts to a flagrant, indefensible, and continuing violation of the First Amendment. Furthermore, after oral argument, I agree completely that we must affirm the judgment of the Court of Appeals for the District of Columbia Circuit and reverse the judgment of the Court of Appeals for the Second Circuit for the reasons stated by my Brothers DOUGLAS and BRENNAN. In my view, it is unfortunate that some of my Brethren are apparently willing to hold that the publication of news may sometimes be enjoined. Such a holding would make a shambles of the First Amendment.

Our Government was launched in 1789 with the adoption of the Constitution. The Bill of Rights, including the First Amendment, followed in 1791. Now, for the first time in the 182 years since the founding of the Republic, the federal courts are asked to hold that the First Amendment does not mean what it says, but rather means that the Government can halt the publication of current news of vital importance to the people of this country.

In seeking injunctions against these newspapers, and in its presentation to the Court, the Executive Branch seems to have forgotten the essential purpose and history of the First Amendment. When the Constitution was adopted, many people strongly opposed it because the document contained no Bill of Rights to safeguard certain basic freedoms.[1] They especially feared that the new powers granted to a central government might be interpreted to permit the government to curtail freedom of religion, press, assembly, and speech. In response to an overwhelming public clamor, James Madison offered a series of amendments to satisfy citizens that these great liberties would remain safe and beyond the power of government to abridge. Madison proposed what later became the First Amendment in three parts, two of which are set out below, and one of which proclaimed:

> "The people shall not be deprived or abridged of their right to speak, to write, or to publish their sentiments, *and the freedom of the press, as one of the great bulwarks of liberty, shall be inviolable.*[2]"

(Emphasis added.) The amendments were offered to curtail and restrict the general powers granted to the Executive, Legislative, and Judicial Branches two years before in the original Constitution. The Bill of Rights changed the original Constitution into a new charter under which no branch of government could abridge the people's freedoms of press, speech, religion, and assembly. Yet the Solicitor General argues and some members of the Court appear to agree that the general powers of the Government adopted in the original Constitution should be interpreted to limit and restrict the specific and emphatic guarantees of the Bill of Rights adopted later. I can imagine no greater perversion of history. Madison and the other Framers of the First Amendment, able men that they were, wrote in language they earnestly believed could never be misunderstood: "Congress shall make no law . . . abridging the freedom . . . of the press. . . ." Both the history and language of the First Amendment support the view that the press must be left free to publish news, whatever the source, without censorship, injunctions, or prior restraints.

In the First Amendment, the Founding Fathers gave the free press the protection it must have to fulfill its essential role in our democracy. The press was to serve the governed, not the governors. The Government's power to censor the press was abolished so that the press would remain forever free to censure the Government. The press was protected so that it could bare the secrets of government and inform the people. Only a free and unrestrained press can effectively expose deception in government. And paramount among the responsibilities of a free press is the duty to prevent any part of the government from deceiving the people and sending them off to distant lands to die of foreign fevers and foreign shot and shell. In my view, far from deserving condemnation for their courageous reporting, the *New York Times*, the *Washington Post*, and other newspapers should be commended for serving the purpose that the Founding Fathers saw so clearly. In revealing the workings of government that led to the Vietnam war, the newspapers nobly did precisely that which the Founders hoped and trusted they would do.

The Government's case here is based on premises entirely different from those that guided the Framers of the First Amendment. The Solicitor General has carefully and emphatically stated:

"Now, Mr. Justice [BLACK], your construction of . . . [the First Amendment] is well known, and I certainly respect it. You say that no law means no law, and that should be obvious. I can only say, Mr. Justice, that to me it is equally obvious that 'no law' does not mean 'no law,' and I would seek to persuade the Court that that is true. . . . [T]here are other parts of the Constitution that grant powers and responsibilities to the Executive, and...the First Amendment was not intended to make it impossible for the Executive to function or to protect the security of the United States.[3]"

And the Government argues in its brief that, in spite of the First Amendment,

"[t]he authority of the Executive Department to protect the nation against publication of information whose disclosure would endanger the national security stems from two interrelated sources: the constitutional power of the President over the conduct of foreign affairs and his authority as Commander-in-Chief.[4]"

`In other words, we are asked to hold that, despite the First Amendment's emphatic command, the Executive Branch, the Congress, and the Judiciary can make laws enjoining publication of current news and abridging freedom of the press in the name of "national security." The Government does not even attempt to rely on any act of Congress. Instead, it makes the bold and dangerously far-reaching contention that the courts should take it upon themselves to "make" a law abridging freedom of the press in the name of equity, presidential power and national security, even when the representatives of the people in Congress have adhered to the command of the First Amendment and refused to make such a law.[5]

To find that the President has "inherent power" to halt the publication of news by resort to the courts would wipe out the First Amendment and destroy the fundamental liberty and security of the very people the Government hopes to make "secure." No one can read the history of the adoption of the First Amendment without being convinced beyond any doubt that it was injunctions like those sought here that Madison and his collaborators intended to outlaw in this Nation for all time.

The word "security" is a broad, vague generality whose contours should not be invoked to abrogate the fundamental law embodied in the First Amendment. The guarding of military and diplomatic secrets at the expense of informed representative government provides no real security for our Republic. The Framers of the First Amendment, fully aware of both the need to defend a new nation and the abuses of the English and Colonial governments, sought to give this new society strength and security by providing that freedom of speech, press, religion, and assembly should not be abridged. This thought was eloquently expressed in 1937 by Mr. Chief Justice Hughes -- great man and great Chief Justice that he was -- when the Court held a man could not be punished for attending a meeting run by Communists.

> "The greater the importance of safeguarding the community from incitements to the overthrow of our institutions by force and violence, the more imperative is the need to preserve inviolate the constitutional rights of free speech, free press and free assembly in order to maintain the opportunity for free political discussion, to the end

that government may be responsive to the will of the people and that changes, if desired, may be obtained by peaceful means. Therein lies the security of the Republic, the very foundation of constitutional government.[6]"

MR. JUSTICE DOUGLAS, with whom MR. JUSTICE BLACK joins, concurring.

While I join the opinion of the Court, I believe it necessary to express my views more fully.

It should be noted at the outset that the First Amendment provides that "Congress shall male no law . . . abridging the freedom of speech, or of the press." That leaves, in my view, no room for governmental restraint on the press.[7]

There is, moreover, no statute barring the publication by the press of the material which the *Times* and the *Post* seek to use. Title 18 U.S.C. § 793(e) provides that

"[w]hoever having unauthorized possession of, access to, or control over any document, writing . . . or information relating to the national defense which information the possessor has reason to believe could be used to the injury of the United States or to the advantage of any foreign nation, willfully communicates . . . the same to any person not entitled to receive it . . . [s]hall be fined not more than $10,000 or imprisoned not more than ten years, or both."

The Government suggests that the word "communicates" is broad enough to encompass publication.

There are eight sections in the chapter on espionage and censorship, §§ 792-799. In three of those eight, "publish" is specifically mentioned: § 794(b) applies to

"Whoever, in time of war, with intent that the same shall be communicated to the enemy, collects, records, publishes, or communicates . . . [the disposition of armed forces]."

Section 797 applies to whoever "reproduces, *publishes*, sells, or gives away" photographs of defense installations.

Section 798, relating to cryptography, applies to whoever: "communicates, furnishes, transmits, or otherwise makes available . . . or *publishes*" the described material.[8] (Emphasis added.)

Thus, it is apparent that Congress was capable of, and did, distinguish between publishing and communication in the various sections of the Espionage Act.

The other evidence that § 793 does not apply to the press is a rejected version of § 793. That version read:

"During any national emergency resulting from a war to which the United States is a party, or from threat of such a war, the President may, by proclamation, declare the existence of such emergency and, by proclamation, prohibit the publishing or communicating of, or the attempting to publish or communicate any information relating to the national defense which, in his judgment, is of such character that it is or might be useful to the enemy." 55 Cong.Rec. 1763.

During the debates in the Senate, the First Amendment was specifically cited, and that provision was defeated. 55 Cong.Rec. 2167.

Judge Gurfein's holding in the *Times* case that this Act does not apply to this case was therefore preeminently sound. Moreover, the Act of September 23, 1950, in amending 18 U.S.C. § 793 states in § 1(b) that:

"Nothing in this Act shall be construed to authorize, require, or establish military or civilian censorship or in any way to limit or infringe upon freedom of the press or of speech as guaranteed by the Constitution of the United States and no regulation shall be promulgated hereunder having that effect." 64 Stat. 987.

Thus, Congress has been faithful to the command of the First Amendment in this area.

So any power that the Government possesses must come from its "inherent power."

The power to wage war is "the power to wage war successfully." See *Hirabayashi v. United States*, 320 U. S. 81, 320 U. S. 93. But the war power stems from a declaration of war. The Constitution by Art. I, § 8, gives Congress, not the President, power "[t]o declare War." Nowhere are presidential wars authorized. We need not decide, therefore, what leveling effect the war power of Congress might have.

These disclosures[9] may have a serious impact. But that is no basis for sanctioning a previous restraint on the press. As stated by Chief Justice Hughes in *Near v. Minnesota*, 283 U. S. 697, 283 U. S. 719-720:

"While reckless assaults upon public men, and efforts to bring obloquy upon those who are endeavoring faithfully to discharge official duties, exert a baleful influence and deserve the severest condemnation in public opinion, it cannot be said that this abuse is greater, and it is believed to be less, than that which characterized the period in which our institutions took shape. Meanwhile, the administration of government has become more complex, the opportunities for malfeasance and corruption have multiplied, crime has grown to most serious propor- tions, and the danger of its protection by unfaithful officials and of the impairment of the fundamental security of life and property by criminal alliances and official neglect, emphasizes the primary need of a vigilant and courageous press, especially in great cities. The fact that the liberty of the press may be abused by miscreant purveyors of scandal does not make any the less necessary the immunity of the press from previous restraint in dealing with official misconduct."

As we stated only the other day in *Organization for a Better Austin v. Keefe*, 402 U. S. 415, 402 U. S. 419, "[a] ny prior restraint on expression comes to this Court with a "heavy presumption" against its constitutional validity."

The Government says that it has inherent powers to go into court and obtain an injunction to protect the national interest, which, in this case, is alleged to be national security.

Near v. Minnesota, 283 U. S. 697, repudiated that expansive doctrine in no uncertain terms.

The dominant purpose of the First Amendment was to prohibit the widespread practice of governmental suppres- sion of embarrassing information. It is common knowledge that the First Amendment was adopted against the wide- spread use of the common law of seditious libel to punish the dissemination of material that is embarrassing to the powers-that-be. See T. Emerson, *The System of Freedom of Expression*, c. V (1970); Z. Chafee, *Free Speech in the United States*, c. XIII (1941). The present cases will, I think, go down in history as the most dramatic illustration of that principle. A debate of large proportions goes on in the

Nation over our posture in Vietnam. That debate antedated the disclosure of the contents of the present documents. The latter are highly relevant to the debate in progress.

Secrecy in government is fundamentally anti-democratic, perpetuating bureaucratic errors. Open debate and discussion of public issues are vital to our national health. On public questions, there should be "uninhibited, robust, and wide-open" debate. *New York Times Co. v. Sullivan*, 376 U. S. 254,376 U. S. 269-270.

I would affirm the judgment of the Court of Appeals in the *Post* case, vacate the stay of the Court of Appeals in the *Times* case, and direct that it affirm the District Court.

The stays in these cases that have been in effect for more than a week constitute a flouting of the principles of the First Amendment as interpreted in *Near v. Minnesota*.

MR. JUSTICE BRENNAN, concurring.

I

I write separately in these cases only to emphasize what should be apparent: that our judgments in the present cases may not be taken to indicate the propriety, in the future, of issuing temporary stays and restraining orders to block the publication of material sought to be suppressed by the Government. So far as I can determine, never before has the United States sought to enjoin a newspaper from pub-lishing information in its possession. The relative novelty of the questions presented, the necessary haste with which decisions were reached, the magnitude of the interests asserted, and the fact that all the parties have concentrated their arguments upon the question whether permanent restraints were proper may have justified at least some of the restraints heretofore imposed in these cases. Certainly it is difficult to fault the several courts below for seeking to assure that the issues here involved were preserved for ultimate review by this Court. But even if it be assumed that some of the interim restraints were proper in the two cases before us, that assumption has no bearing upon the propriety of similar judicial action in the future. To begin with, there has now been ample time for reflection and judgment; whatever values there may be in the preservation of novel questions for appellate review may not support any restraints in the future. More important, the First Amendment stands as an absolute bar to the imposition of judicial restraints in circumstances of the kind presented by these cases.

II

The error that has pervaded these cases from the outset was the granting of any injunctive relief whatsoever, interim or otherwise. The entire thrust of the Government's claim throughout these cases has been that publication of the material sought to be enjoined "could," or "might," or "may" prejudice the national interest in various ways. But the First Amendment tolerates absolutely no prior judicial restraints of the press predicated upon surmise or conjecture that untoward consequences may result.* Our cases, it is true, have indicated that there is a single, extremely narrow class of cases in which the First Amendment's ban on prior judicial restraint may be overridden. Our cases have thus far indicated that such cases may arise only when the Nation "is at war," *Schenck v. United States*, 249 U. S. 47, 249 U. S. 52 (1919), during which times

"[n]o one would question but that a government
might prevent actual obstruction to its recruiting
service or the publication of the sailing dates of
transports or the number and location of troops."

Near v. Minnesota, 283 U. S. 697, 283 U. S. 716 (1931).
Even if the present world situation were assumed to be
tantamount to a time of war, or if the power of presently
available armaments would justify even in peacetime
the suppression of information that would set in motion
a nuclear holocaust, in neither of these actions has the
Government presented or even alleged that publication of items from or based upon the material at issue
would cause the happening of an event of that nature.
"[T]he chief purpose of [the First Amendment's] guaranty [is] to prevent previous restraints upon publication."
Near v. Minnesota, supra, at 283 U. S. 713. Thus, only
governmental allegation and proof that publication must
inevitably, directly, and immediately cause the occur-
rence of an event kindred to imperiling the safety of a
transport already at sea can support even the issuance of
an interim restraining order. In no event may mere conclusions be sufficient, for if the Executive Branch seeks judicial aid in preventing publication, it must inevitably submit
the basis upon which that aid is sought to scrutiny by the
judiciary. And, therefore, every restraint issued in this
case, whatever its form, has violated the First Amendment
-- and not less so because that restraint was justified as
necessary to afford the courts an opportunity to examine
the claim more thoroughly. Unless and until the Government has clearly made out its case, the First Amendment
commands that no injunction may issue.

MR. JUSTICE STEWART, with whom MR. JUSTICE WHITE joins, concurring.

In the governmental structure created by our Constitution, the Executive is endowed with enormous power in the two related areas of national defense and international relations. This power, largely unchecked by the Legislative[10] and Judicial[11] branches, has been pressed to the very hilt since the advent of the nuclear missile age. For better or for worse, the simple fact is that a President of the United States possesses vastly greater constitutional independence in these two vital areas of power than does, say, a prime minister of a country with a parliamentary form of government.

In the absence of the governmental checks and balances present in other areas of our national life, the only effective restraint upon executive policy and power in the areas of national defense and international affairs may lie in an enlightened citizenry -- in an informed and critical public opinion which alone can here protect the values of democratic government. For this reason, it is perhaps here that a press that is alert, aware, and free most vitally serves the basic purpose of the First Amendment. For, without an informed and free press, there cannot be an enlightened people.

Yet it is elementary that the successful conduct of international diplomacy and the maintenance of an effective national defense require both confidentiality and secrecy. Other nations can hardly deal with this Nation in an atmosphere of mutual trust unless they can be assured that their confidences will be kept. And, within our own executive departments, the development of considered and intelligent international policies would be impossible if those charged with their formulation could not communicate with each other freely, frankly, and in confidence. In the area of basic national defense, the frequent need for absolute secrecy is, of course, self-evident.

I think there can be but one answer to this dilemma, if dilemma it be. The responsibility must be where the power is.[12] If the Constitution gives the Executive a large degree of unshared power in the conduct of foreign affairs and the maintenance of our national defense, then, under the Constitution, the Executive must have the largely unshared duty to determine and preserve the degree of internal security necessary to exercise that power successfully. It is an awesome responsibility, requiring judgment and wisdom of a high order. I should suppose that moral, political, and practical considerations would dictate that a very first principle of that wisdom would be an insistence upon avoiding secrecy for its own sake. For when everything is classified, then nothing is classified, and the system becomes one to be disregarded by the cynical or the careless, and to be manipulated by those intent on self-protection or self-promotion. I should suppose, in short, that the hallmark of a truly effective internal security system would be the maximum possible disclosure, recognizing that secrecy can best be preserved only when credibility is truly maintained. But, be that as it may, it is clear to me that it is the constitutional duty of the Executive -- as a matter of sovereign prerogative, and not as a matter of law as the courts know law -- through the promulgation and enforcement of executive regulations, to protect the confidentiality necessary to carry out its responsibilities in the fields of international relations and national defense.

This is not to say that Congress and the courts have no role to play. Undoubtedly, Congress has the power to enact specific and appropriate criminal laws to protect government property and preserve government secrets. Congress has passed such laws, and several of them are of very colorable relevance to the apparent circumstances of these cases. And if a criminal prosecution is instituted, it will be the responsibility of the courts to decide the applicability of the criminal law under which the charge is brought. Moreover, if Congress should pass a specific law authorizing civil proceedings in this field, the courts would likewise have the duty to decide the constitutionality of such a law, as well as its applicability to the facts proved.

But in the cases before us, we are asked neither to construe specific regulations nor to apply specific laws. We are asked, instead, to perform a function that the Constitution gave to the Executive, not the Judiciary. We are asked, quite simply, to prevent the publication by two newspapers of material that the Executive Branch insists should not, in the national interest, be published. I am convinced that the Executive is correct with respect to some of the documents involved. But I cannot say that disclosure of any of them will surely result in direct, immediate, and irreparable damage to our Nation or its people. That being so, there can under the First Amendment be but one judicial resolution of the issues before us. I join the judgments of the Court.

[...]

119

MR. CHIEF JUSTICE BURGER, dissenting.

So clear are the constitutional limitations on prior restraint against expression that, from the time of *Near v. Minnesota*, 283 U. S. 697 (1931), until recently in *Organization for a Better Austin v. Keefe*, 402 U. S. 415 (1971), we have had little occasion to be concerned with cases involving prior restraints against news reporting on matters of public interest. There is, therefore, little variation among the members of the Court in terms of resistance to prior restraints against publication. Adherence to this basic constitutional principle, however, does not make these cases simple. In these cases, the imperative of a free and unfettered press comes into collision with another imperative, the effective functioning of a complex modern government, and, specifically, the effective exercise of certain constitutional powers of the Executive. Only those who view the First Amendment as an absolute in all circumstances -- a view I respect, but reject -- can find such cases as these to be simple or easy.

These cases are not simple for another and more immediate reason. We do not know the facts of the cases. No District Judge knew all the facts. No Court of Appeals judge knew all the facts. No member of this Court knows all the facts.

Why are we in this posture, in which only those judges to whom the First Amendment is absolute and permits of no restraint in any circumstances or for any reason, are really in a position to act?

I suggest we are in this posture because these cases have been conducted in unseemly haste. MR.

JUSTICE HARLAN covers the chronology of events demonstrating the hectic pressures under which these cases have been processed, and I need not restate them. The prompt setting of these cases reflects our universal abhorrence of prior restraint. But prompt judicial action does not mean unjudicial haste.

Here, moreover, the frenetic haste is due in large part to the manner in which the *Times* proceeded from the date it obtained the purloined documents. It seems reasonably clear now that the haste precluded reasonable and deliberate judicial treatment of these cases, and was not warranted. The precipitate action of this Court aborting trials not yet completed is not the kind of judicial conduct that ought to attend the disposition of a great issue.

The newspapers make a derivative claim under the First Amendment; they denominate this right as the public "right to know"; by implication, the *Times* asserts a sole trusteeship of that right by virtue of its journalistic "scoop." The right is asserted as an absolute. Of course, the First Amendment right itself is not an absolute, as Justice Holmes so long ago pointed out in his aphorism concerning the right to shout "fire" in a crowded theater if there was no fire. There are other exceptions, some of which Chief Justice Hughes mentioned by way of example in *Near v. Minnesota*. There are no doubt other exceptions no one has had occasion to describe or discuss. Conceivably, such exceptions may be lurking in these cases and, would have been flushed had they been properly considered in the trial courts, free from unwarranted deadlines and frenetic pressures. An issue of this importance should be tried and heard in a judicial atmosphere conducive to thoughtful, reflective deliberation, especially when haste, in terms of hours, is unwarranted in light of the long period the *Times*, by its own choice, deferred publication.[13]

It is not disputed that the *Times* has had unauthorized possession of the documents for three to four months, during which it has had its expert analysts studying them, presumably digesting them and preparing the material for publication. During all of this time, the *Times*, presumably in its capacity as trustee of the public's "right to know," has held up publication for purposes it considered proper, and thus public knowledge was delayed. No doubt this was for a good reason; the analysis of 7,000 pages of complex material drawn from a vastly greater volume of material would inevitably take time, and the writing of good news stories takes time. But why should the United States Government, from whom this information was illegally acquired by someone, along with all the counsel, trial judges, and appellate judges be placed under needless pressure? After these months of deferral, the alleged "right to know" has somehow and suddenly become a right that must be vindicated instanter.

Would it have been unreasonable, since the newspaper could anticipate the Government's objections to release of secret material, to give the Government an opportunity to review the entire collection and determine whether agreement could be reached on publication? Stolen or not, if security was not, in fact, jeopardized, much of the material could no doubt have been declassified, since it spans a period ending in 1968. With such an approach -- one that great newspapers have in the past practiced and stated editorially to be the duty of an honorable press -- the newspapers and Government might well have narrowed the area of disagreement as to what was and was not publishable, leaving the remainder to be resolved in orderly litigation, if necessary. To me, it is hardly believable that a newspaper long regarded as a great institution in American life would fail to perform one of the basic and simple duties of every citizen with respect to the discovery or possession of stolen property or secret government documents. That duty, I had thought -- perhaps naively -- was to report forthwith, to responsible public officers. This duty rests on taxi drivers, Justices, and the *New York Times*. The course followed by the *Times*, whether so calculated or not, removed any possibility of orderly litigation of the issue. If the action of the judges up to now has been correct, that result is sheer happenstance.

Our grant of the writ of certiorari before final judgment in the *Times* case aborted the trial in the District Court before it had made a complete record pursuant to the mandate of the Court of Appeals for the Second Circuit.[14]

The consequence of all this melancholy series of events is that we literally do not know what we are acting on. As I see it, we have been forced to deal with litigation concerning rights of great magnitude without an adequate record, and surely without time for adequate treatment either in the prior proceedings or in this Court. It is interesting to note that counsel on both sides, in oral argument before this Court, were frequently unable to respond to questions on factual points. Not surprisingly, they pointed out that they had been working literally "around the clock," and simply were unable to review the documents that give rise to these cases and were not familiar with them. This Court is in no better posture.

I agree generally with MR. JUSTICE HARLAN and MR. JUSTICE BLACKMUN, but I am not prepared to reach the merits.[15]

I would affirm the Court of Appeals for the Second Circuit and allow the District Court to complete the trial aborted by our grant of certiorari, meanwhile preserving the status quo in the *Post* case. I would direct that the District Court, on remand, give priority to the *Times* case to the exclusion of all other business of that court, but I would not set arbitrary deadlines.

I should add that I am in general agreement with much of what MR. JUSTICE WHITE has expressed with respect to penal sanctions concerning communication or retention of documents or information relating to the national defense.

We all crave speedier judicial processes, but, when judges are pressured, as in these cases, the result is a parody of the judicial function.

MR. JUSTICE HARLAN, with whom THE CHIEF JUSTICE and MR. JUSTICE BLACKMUN join, dissenting.

These cases forcefully call to mind the wise admonition of Mr. Justice Holmes, dissenting in *Northern Securities Co. v. United States*, 193 U. S. 197, 193 U. S. 400-401 (1904):

> "Great cases, like hard cases, make bad law. For great cases are called great not by reason of their real importance in shaping the law of the future, but because of some accident of immediate over- whelming interest which appeals to the feelings and distorts the judgment. These immediate inter- ests exercise a kind of hydraulic pressure which

makes what previously was clear seem doubtful, and before which even well settled principles of law will bend."

With all respect, I consider that the Court has been almost irresponsibly feverish in dealing with these cases.

Both the Court of Appeals for the Second Circuit and the Court of Appeals for the District of Columbia Circuit rendered judgment on June 23. *The New York Times'* petition for certiorari, its motion for accelerated consideration thereof, and its application for interim relief were filed in this Court on June 24 at about 11 a.m. The application of the United States for interim relief in the *Post* case was also filed here on June 24 at about 7:15 p.m. This Court's order setting a hearing before us on June 26 at 11 a.m., a course which I joined only to avoid the possibility of even more peremptory action by the Court, was issued less than 24 hours before. The record in the *Post* case was filed with the Clerk shortly before 1 p.m. on June 25; the record in the *Times* case did not arrive until 7 or 8 o'clock that same night. The briefs of the parties were received less than two hours before argument on June 26.

This frenzied train of events took place in the name of the presumption against prior restraints created by the First Amendment. Due regard for the extraordinarily important and difficult questions involved in these litigations should have led the Court to shun such a precipitate timetable. In order to decide the merits of these cases properly, some or all of the following questions should have been faced:

1. Whether the Attorney General is authorized to bring these suits in the name of the *United States*. Compare *In re Debs*, 158 U. S. 564 (1895), with *Youngstown*

Sheet & Tube Co. v. Sawyer, 343 U. S. 579 (1952). This question involves as well the construction and validity of a singularly opaque statute -- the Espionage Act, 18 U.S.C. § 793(e).

2. Whether the First Amendment permits the federal courts to enjoin publication of stories which would present a serious threat to national security. See *Near v. Minnesota*, 283 U. S. 697, 283 U. S. 716 (1931) (dictum).

3. Whether the threat to publish highly secret documents is of itself a sufficient implication of national security to justify an injunction on the theory that, regardless of the contents of the documents, harm enough results simply from the demonstration of such a breach of secrecy.

4. Whether the unauthorized disclosure of any of these particular documents would seriously impair the national security.

5. What weight should be given to the opinion of high officers in the Executive Branch of the Government with respect to questions 3 and 4.

6. Whether the newspapers are entitled to retain and use the documents notwithstanding the seemingly uncontested facts that the documents, or the originals of which they are duplicates, were purloined from the Government's possession, and that the newspapers received them with knowledge that they had been feloniously acquired. *Cf. Liberty Lobby, Inc. v. Pearson*, 129 U.S.App.D.C. 74, 390 F.2d 489 (1967, amended 1968).

7. Whether the threatened harm to the national security or the Government's possessory interest in the documents justifies the issuance of an injunction against publication in light of --

   a. The strong First Amendment policy against prior restraints on publication;

   b. The doctrine against enjoining conduct in violation of criminal statutes; and

   c. The extent to which the materials at issue have apparently already been otherwise disseminated.

These are difficult questions of fact, of law, and of judgment; the potential consequences of erroneous decision are enormous. The time which has been available to us, to the lower courts,* and to the parties has been wholly inadequate for giving these cases the kind of consideration they deserve. It is a reflection on the stability of the judicial process that these great issues -- as important as any that have arisen during my time on the Court -- should have been decided under the pressures engendered by the torrent of publicity that has attended these litigations from their inception.

Forced as I am to reach the merits of these cases, I dissent from the opinion and judgments of the Court. Within the severe limitations imposed by the time constraints under which I have been required to operate, I can only state my reasons in telescoped form, even though, in different circumstances, I would have felt constrained to deal with the cases in the fuller sweep indicated above.

It is a sufficient basis for affirming the Court of Appeals for the Second Circuit in the *Times* litigation to observe that its order must rest on the conclusion that, because of the time elements the Government had not been given an adequate opportunity to present its case to the District Court. At the least this conclusion was not an abuse of discretion.

In the *Post* litigation, the Government had more time to prepare; this was apparently the basis for the refusal of the Court of Appeals for the District of Columbia Circuit on rehearing to conform its judgment to that of the Second Circuit. But I think there is another and more fundamental reason why this judgment cannot stand -- a reason which also furnishes an additional ground for not reinstating the judgment of the District Court in the *Times* litigation, set aside by the Court of Appeals. It is plain to me that the scope of the judicial function in passing upon the activities of the Executive Branch of the Government in the field of foreign affairs is very narrowly restricted. This view is, I think, dictated by the concept of separation of powers upon which our constitutional system rests.

In a speech on the floor of the House of Representatives, Chief Justice John Marshall, then a member of that body, stated:

> "The President is the sole organ of the nation in its external relations, and its sole representative with foreign nations." 10 Annals of Cong. 613 (1800).

From that time, shortly after the founding of the Nation, to this, there has been no substantial challenge to this description of the scope of executive power. *See United States v. Curtiss-Wright Corp.*, 299 U. S. 304, 299 U. S. 319-321 (1936), collecting authorities.

From this constitutional primacy in the field of foreign affairs, it seems to me that certain conclusions necessarily follow. Some of these were stated concisely by President Washington, declining the request of the House of Representatives for the papers leading up to the negotiation of the Jay Treaty:

> "The nature of foreign negotiations requires caution, and their success must often depend on secrecy; and even when brought to a conclusion, a full disclosure of all the measures, demands, or eventual concessions which may have been proposed or contemplated would be extremely impolitic; for this might have a pernicious influence on future negotiations, or produce immediate inconveniences, perhaps danger and mischief, in relation to other powers." 1 J. Richardson, Messages and Papers of the Presidents 194-195 (1896).

The power to evaluate the "pernicious influence" of premature disclosure is not, however, lodged in the Executive alone. I agree that, in performance of its duty to protect the values of the First Amendment against political pressures, the judiciary must review the initial Executive determination to the point of satisfying itself that the subject matter of the dispute does lie within the proper compass of the President's foreign relations power. Constitutional considerations forbid "a complete abandonment of judicial control." Cf. *United States v. Reynolds*, 345 U. S. 1, 345 U. S. 8 (1953). Moreover, the judiciary may properly insist that the determination that disclosure of the subject matter would irreparably impair the national security be made by the head of the Executive Department concerned -- here, the Secretary of State or the Secretary of Defense -- after actual personal consideration by that officer. This safeguard is required in the analogous area of executive claims of privilege for secrets of state. *See id.* at 345 U. S. 8 and n. 20; *Duncan v. Cammell, Laird Co.*, [1942] A.C. 624, 638 (House of Lords).

But, in my judgment, the judiciary may not properly go beyond these two inquiries and redetermine for itself the probable impact of disclosure on the national security.

> "[T]he very nature of executive decisions as to foreign policy is political, not judicial. Such decisions are wholly confided by our Constitution to the political departments of the government, Executive and Legislative. They are delicate, complex, and involve large elements of prophecy. They are and should be undertaken only by those directly responsible to the people whose welfare they advance or imperil. They are decisions of a kind for which the Judiciary has neither aptitude, facilities nor responsibility, and which has long been held to belong in the domain of political power not subject to judicial intrusion or inquiry." *Chicago & Southern Air Lines v. Waterman Steamship Corp.*, 333 U. S. 103, 333 U. S. 111 (1948) (Jackson, J.).

Even if there is some room for the judiciary to override the executive determination, it is plain that the scope of review must be exceedingly narrow. I can see no indication in the opinions of either the District Court or the Court of Appeals in the *Post* litigation that the conclusions of the Executive were given even the deference owing to an administrative agency, much less that owing to a co-equal branch of the Government operating within the field of its constitutional prerogative.

Accordingly, I would vacate the judgment of the Court of Appeals for the District of Columbia Circuit on this ground, and remand the case for further proceedings in the District Court. Before the commencement of such further proceedings, due opportunity should be afforded the Government for procuring from the Secretary of State or the Secretary of Defense or both an expression of their views on the issue of national security. The ensuing review by the District Court should be in accordance with the views expressed in this opinion. And, for the reasons stated above, I would affirm the judgment of the Court of Appeals for the Second Circuit.

Pending further hearings in each case conducted under the appropriate ground rules, I would continue the restraints on publication. I cannot believe that the doctrine prohibiting prior restraints reaches to the point of preventing courts from maintaining the status quo long enough to act responsibly in matters of such national importance as those involved here.

MR. JUSTICE BLACKMUN, dissenting.

I join MR. JUSTICE HARLAN in his dissent. I also am in substantial accord with much that MR. JUSTICE WHITE says, by way of admonition, in the latter part of his opinion.

At this point, the focus is on only the comparatively few documents specified by the Government as critical. So far as the other material -- vast in amount -- is concerned, let it be published and published forthwith if the newspapers, once the strain is gone and the sensationalism is eased, still feel the urge so to do.

But we are concerned here with the few documents specified from the 47 volumes. Almost 70 years ago, Mr. Justice Holmes, dissenting in a celebrated case, observed:

> "Great cases, like hard cases, make bad law. For great cases are called great not by reason of their real importance in shaping the law of the future, but because of some accident of immediate overwhelming interest which appeals to the feelings and distorts the judgment. These immediate interests exercise a kind of hydraulic pressure. . . ." *Northen Securities Co. v. United States*, 193 U. S. 197, 193 U. S. 400-401 (1904).

The present cases, if not great, are at least unusual in their posture and implications, and the Holmes observation certainly has pertinent application.

The New York Times clandestinely devoted a period of three months to examining the 47 volumes that came into its unauthorized possession. Once it had begun publication of material from those volumes, the New York case now before us emerged. It immediately assumed, and ever since has maintained, a frenetic pace and character. Seemingly, once publication started, the material could not be made public fast enough. Seemingly, from then on, every deferral or delay, by restraint or otherwise, was abhorrent, and was to be deemed violative of the First Amendment and of the public's "right immediately to know." Yet that newspaper stood before us at oral argument and professed criticism of the Government for not lodging its protest earlier than by a Monday telegram following the initial Sunday publication.

The District of Columbia case is much the same.

Two federal district courts, two United States courts of appeals, and this Court -- within a period of less than three weeks from inception until today -- have been pressed into hurried decision of profound constitutional issues on inadequately developed and largely assumed facts without the careful deliberation that, one would hope, should characterize the American judicial process. There has been much writing about the law and little knowledge and less digestion of the facts. In the New York case, the judges, both trial and appellate, had not yet examined the basic material when the case was brought here. In the District of Columbia case, little more was done, and what was accomplished in this respect was only on required remand, with the Washington *Post*, on the excuse that it was trying to protect its source of information, initially refusing to reveal what material it actually possessed, and with the District Court forced to make assumptions as to that possession.

With such respect as may be due to the contrary view, this, in my opinion, is not the way to try a lawsuit of this magnitude and asserted importance. It is not the way for federal courts to adjudicate, and to be required to adjudicate, issues that allegedly concern the Nation's vital welfare. The country would be none the worse off were the cases tried quickly, to be sure, but in the customary and properly deliberative manner. The most recent of the material, it is said, dates no later than 1968, already about three years ago, and the *Times* itself took three months to formulate its plan of procedure and, thus, deprived its public for that period.

The First Amendment, after all, is only one part of an entire Constitution. Article II of the great document vests in the Executive Branch primary power over the conduct of foreign affairs, and places in that branch the responsibility for the Nation's safety. Each provision of the Constitution is important, and I cannot subscribe to a doctrine of unlimited absolutism for the First Amendment at the cost of downgrading other provisions. First Amendment absolutism has never commanded a majority of this Court. *See,* for example, *Near v. Minnesota*, 283 U. S. 697, 283 U. S. 708 (1931), and *Schenck v. United States*, 249 U. S. 47, 249 U. S. 52 (1919). What is needed here is a weighing, upon properly developed standards, of the broad right of the press to print and of the very narrow right of the Government to prevent. Such standards are not yet developed. The parties here are in disagreement as to what those standards should be. But even the newspapers concede that there are situations where restraint is in order and is constitutional. Mr. Justice Holmes gave us a suggestion when he said in *Schenck*,

> "It is a question of proximity and degree. When a nation is at war, many things that might be said in time of peace are such a hindrance to its effort that their utterance will not be endured so long as men fight and that no Court could regard them as protected by any constitutional right." 249 U.S. at 249 U. S. 52.

I therefore would remand these cases to be developed expeditiously, of course, but on a schedule permitting the orderly presentation of evidence from both sides, with the use of discovery, if necessary, as authorized by the rules, and with the preparation of briefs, oral argument, and court opinions of a quality better than has been seen to this point. In making this last statement, I criticize no lawyer or judge. I know from past personal experience the agony of time pressure in the preparation of litigation. But these cases and the issues involved and the courts, including this one, deserve better than has been produced thus far.

It may well be that, if these cases were allowed to develop as they should be developed, and to be tried as lawyers should try them and as courts should hear them, free of pressure and panic and sensationalism, other light would be shed on the situation, and contrary considerations, for me, might prevail. But that is not the present posture of the litigation.

The Court, however, decides the cases today the other way. I therefore add one final comment.

I strongly urge, and sincerely hope, that these two newspapers will be fully aware of their ultimate responsibilities to the United States of America. Judge Wilkey, dissenting in the District of Columbia case, after a review of only the affidavits before his court (the basic papers had not then been made available by either party), concluded that there were a number of examples of documents that, if in the possession of the *Post* and if published, "could clearly result in great harm to the nation," and he defined "harm" to mean "the death of soldiers, the destruction of alliances, the greatly increased difficulty of negotiation with our enemies, the inability of our diplomats to negotiate. . . ."

I, for one, have now been able to give at least some cursory study not only to the affidavits, but to the material itself. I regret to say that, from this examination, I fear that Judge Wilkey's statements have possible foundation. I therefore share his concern. I hope that damage has not already been done. If, however, damage has been done, and if, with the Court's action today, these newspapers proceed to publish the critical documents and there results therefrom "the death of soldiers, the destruction of alliances, the greatly increased difficulty of negotiation with our enemies, the inability of our diplomats to negotiate," to which list I might add the factors of prolongation of the war and of further delay in the freeing of United States prisoners, then the Nation's people will know where the responsibility for these sad consequences rests.

1. What responsibilities does the press have to protect national interest?

2. How do times of war complicate the way courts handle freedom of the press cases?

BRANZBURG V. HAYES, UNITED STATES SUPREME COURT, JUNE 29, 1972

The First Amendment does not relieve a newspaper reporter of the obligation that all citizens have to respond to a grand jury subpoena and answer questions relevant to a criminal investigation, and therefore the Amendment does not afford him a constitutional testimonial privilege for an agreement he makes to conceal facts relevant to a grand jury's investigation of a crime or to conceal the criminal conduct of his source or evidence thereof. Pp. 408 U. S. 679-709.

No. 705, 461 S.W.2d 345, and Kentucky Court of Appeals judgment in unreported case of *Branzburg v. Meigs*, and No. 70-94, 358 Mass. 604, 266 N.E.2d 297, affirmed; No. 70-57, 434 F.2d 1081, reversed.

WHITE, J., wrote the opinion of the Court, in which BURGER, C.J., and BLACKMUN, POWELL, and REHNQUIST,

JJ., joined. POWELL, J., filed a concurring opinion, post, p. 408 U. S. 709. DOUGLAS, J., filed a dissenting opinion, post, p. 408 U. S. 711. STEWART, J., filed a dissenting opinion, in which BRENNAN and MARSHALL, JJ., joined, post, p. 408 U. S. 725.

Opinion of the Court by MR. JUSTICE WHITE, announced by THE CHIEF JUSTICE.

The issue in these cases is whether requiring newsmen to appear and testify before state or federal grand juries abridges the freedom of speech and press guaranteed by the First Amendment. We hold that it does not.

I

The writ of certiorari in No. 70-85, *Branzburg v. Hayes and Meigs*, brings before us two judgments of the Kentucky Court of Appeals, both involving petitioner Branzburg, a staff reporter for the Courier-Journal, a daily newspaper published in Louisville, Kentucky.

On November 15, 1969, the Courier-Journal carried a story under petitioner's by-line describing in detail his observations of two young residents of Jefferson County synthesizing hashish from marihuana, an activity which, they asserted, earned them about $5,000 in three weeks. The article included a photograph of a pair of hands working above a laboratory table on which was a substance identified by the caption as hashish. The article stated that petitioner had promised not to reveal the identity of the two hashish makers.[1] Petitioner was shortly subpoenaed by the Jefferson County grand jury; he appeared, but refused to identify the individuals he had seen possessing marihuana or the persons he had seen making hashish from marihuana.[2] A state trial court judge[3] ordered petitioner to answer these questions and rejected his contention that the Kentucky reporters' privilege statute, Ky.Rev.Stat. § 421.100 (1962)[4] the First Amendment of the United States Constitution, or §§ 1, 2, and 8 of the Kentucky Constitution authorized his refusal to answer. Petitioner then sought prohibition and mandamus in the Kentucky Court of Appeals on the same ground, but the Court of Appeals denied the petition. *Branzburg v. Pound*, 461 S.W.2d 345 (1970), as modified on denial of rehearing, Jan. 22, 1971. It held that petitioner had abandoned his First Amendment argument in a supplemental memorandum he had filed and tacitly rejected his argument based on the Kentucky Constitution. It also construed Ky.Rev.Stat. § 421.100 as affording a newsman the privilege of refusing to divulge the identity of an informant who supplied him with information, but held that the statute did not permit a reporter to refuse to testify about events he had observed personally, including the identities of those persons he had observed.

The second case involving petitioner Branzburg arose out of his later story published on January 10, 1971, which described in detail the use of drugs in Frankfort, Kentucky. The article reported that, in order to provide a comprehensive survey of the "drug scene" in Frankfort, petitioner had "spent two weeks interviewing several dozen drug users in the capital city," and had seen some of them smoking marihuana. A number of conversations with and observations of several unnamed drug users were recounted. Subpoenaed to appear before a Franklin County grand jury "to testify in the matter of violation of statutes concerning use and sale of drugs," petitioner Branzburg moved to quash the summons;[5] the motion was denied, although an order was issued protecting Branzburg from revealing "confidential associations, sources or information" but requiring that he "answer any questions which concern or pertain to any criminal act, the commission of which was actually observed by [him]." Prior to the time he was slated to appear before the grand jury, petitioner sought mandamus and prohibition from the Kentucky Court of Appeals, arguing that, if he were forced to go before the grand jury or to answer questions regarding the identity of informants or disclose information given to him in confidence, his effectiveness as a reporter would be greatly damaged. The Court of Appeals once again denied the requested writs, reaffirming its construction of Ky.Rev.Stat. § 421.100, and rejecting petitioner's claim of a First Amendment privilege. It distinguished *Caldwell v. United States*, 434 F.2d 1081 (CA9 1970), and it also announced its "misgivings" about that decision, asserting that it represented "a drastic departure from the generally recognized rule that the sources of information of a newspaper reporter are not privileged under the First Amendment." It characterized petitioner's fear that his ability to obtain news would be destroyed as

> "so tenuous that it does not, in the opinion of this court, present an issue of abridgement of the freedom of the press within the meaning of that term as used in the Constitution of the United States."

Petitioner sought a writ of certiorari to review both judgments of the Kentucky Court of Appeals, and we granted the writ.[6] 402 U.S. 942 (1971. In *re Pappas*, No. 70-94, originated when petitioner Pappas, a television newsman-photographer working out of the Providence,

Rhode Island, office of a New Bedford, Massachusetts, television station, was called to New Bedford on July 30, 1970, to report on civil disorders there which involved fires and other turmoil. He intended to cover a Black Panther news conference at that group's headquarters in a boarded-up store. Petitioner found the streets around the store barricaded, but he ultimately gained entrance to the area and recorded and photographed a prepared statement read by one of the Black Panther leaders at about 3 p.m.[7] He then asked for and received permission to reenter the area. Returning at about 9 o'clock, he was allowed to enter and remain inside Panther headquarters. As a condition of entry, Pappas agreed not to disclose anything he saw or heard inside the store except an anticipated police raid, which Pappas, "on his own," was free to photograph and report as he wished. Pappas stayed inside the headquarters for about three hours, but there was no police raid, and petitioner wrote no story and did not otherwise reveal what had occurred in the store while he was there. Two months later, petitioner was summoned before the Bristol County Grand Jury and appeared, answered questions as to his name, address, employment, and what he had seen and heard outside Panther headquarters, but refused to answer any questions about what had taken place inside headquarters while he was there, claiming that the First Amendment afforded him a privilege to protect confidential informants and their information. A second summons was then served upon him, again directing him to appear before the grand jury and "to give such evidence as he knows relating to any matters which may be inquired of on behalf of the Commonwealth before . . . the Grand Jury." His motion to quash on First Amendment and other grounds was denied by the trial judge who, noting the absence of a statutory newsman's privilege in Massachusetts, ruled that petitioner had no constitutional privilege to refuse to divulge to the grand jury what he had seen and heard, including the identity of persons he had observed. The case was reported for decision to the Supreme Judicial Court of Massachusetts.[8] The record there did not include a transcript of the hearing on the motion to quash, nor did it reveal the specific questions petitioner had refused to answer, the expected nature of his testimony, the nature of the grand jury investigation, or the likelihood of the grand jury's securing the information it sought from petitioner by other means.[9] The Supreme Judicial Court, however, took

> "judicial notice that, in July, 1970, there were serious civil disorders in New Bedford, which involved street barricades, exclusion of the public from certain streets, fires, and similar turmoil. We were told at the arguments that there was gunfire in certain streets. We assume that the grand jury investigation was an appropriate effort to discover and indict those responsible for criminal acts." 358 Mass. 604, 607, 266 N.E.2d 297, 299 (1971).

The court then reaffirmed prior Massachusetts holdings that testimonial privileges were "exceptional" and "limited," stating that "[t]he principle that the public has a right to every man's evidence'" had usually been preferred, in the Commonwealth, to countervailing interests. *Ibid*. The court rejected the holding of the Ninth Circuit in *Caldwell v. United States, supra*, and

"adhere[d] to the view that there exists no constitutional newsman's privilege, either qualified or absolute, to

refuse to appear and testify before a court or grand jury.[10]"
358 Mass. at 612, 266 N.E.2d at 302-303.

Any adverse effect upon the free dissemination of news by virtue of petitioner's being called to testify was deemed to be only "indirect, theoretical, and uncertain." *Id.* at 612, 266 N.E.2d at 302. The court concluded that

"[t]he obligation of newsmen . . . is that of every citizen . . . to appear when summoned, with relevant written or other material when required, and to answer relevant and reasonable inquiries." *Id.* at 612, 266 N.E.2d at 303.

The court nevertheless noted that grand juries were subject to supervision by the presiding judge, who had the duty "to prevent oppressive, unnecessary, irrelevant, and other improper inquiry and investigation," ibid., to insure that a witness' Fifth Amendment rights were not infringed, and to assess the propriety, necessity, and pertinence of the probable testimony to the investigation in progress.[11] The burden was deemed to be on the witness to establish the impropriety of the summons or the questions asked. The denial of the motion to quash was affirmed, and we granted a writ of certiorari to petitioner Pappas. 402 U.S. 942 (1971).

United States v. Caldwell, No. 70-57, arose from subpoenas issued by a federal grand jury in the Northern District of California to respondent Earl Caldwell, a reporter for the *New York Times* assigned to cover the Black Panther Party and other black militant groups. A subpoena duces tecum was served on respondent on February 2, 1970, ordering him to appear before the grand jury to testify and to bring with him notes and tape recordings of interviews given him for publication by officers and spokesmen of the Black Panther Party concerning the aims, purposes, and activities of that organization.[12] Respondent objected to the scope of this subpoena, and an agreement between his counsel and the Government attorneys resulted in a continuance. A second subpoena, served on March 16, omitted the documentary requirement and simply ordered Caldwell "to appear . . . to testify before the Grand Jury." Respondent and his employer, the *New York Times*,[13] moved to quash on the ground that the unlimited breadth of the subpoenas and the fact that Caldwell would have to appear in secret before the grand jury would destroy his working relationship with the Black Panther Party and "suppress vital First Amendment freedoms . . . by driving a wedge of distrust and silence between the news media and the militants." App. 7. Respondent argued that "so drastic an incursion upon First Amendment freedoms" should not be permitted "in the absence of a compelling governmental interest -- not shown here -- in requiring Mr. Caldwell's appearance before the grand jury." *Ibid.* The motion was supported by amicus curiae memoranda from other publishing concerns and by affidavits from newsmen asserting the unfavorable impact on news sources of requiring reporters to appear before grand juries. The Government filed three memoranda in opposition to the motion to quash, each supported by affidavits. These documents stated that the grand jury was investigating, among other things, possible violations of a number of criminal statutes, including 18 U.S.C. § 871 (threats against the President), 18 U.S.C. § 1751 (assassination, attempts to assassinate, conspiracy to assassinate the President), 18 U.S.C. § 231 (civil disorders), 18 U.S.C. § 2101 (interstate travel to incite a riot), and 18 U.S.C. § 1341 (mail frauds and swindles). It was recited that, on November 15, 1969, an officer of the Black Panther Party made a publicly televised speech in which he had declared that "[w]e will kill Richard Nixon" and that this threat had been repeated in three subsequent issues of the Party newspaper. App. 66, 77. Also referred to were various writings by Caldwell about the Black Panther Party, including an article published in the *New York Times* on December 14, 1969, stating that "[i]n their role as the vanguard in a revolutionary struggle, the Panthers have picked up guns," and quoting the Chief of Staff of the Party as declaring:

> "We advocate the very direct overthrow of the Government by way of force and violence. By picking up guns and moving against it because we recognize it as being oppressive and, in recognizing that, we know that the only solution to it is armed struggle [sic]." App. 62.

The Government also stated that the Chief of Staff of the Party had been indicted by the grand jury on December 3, 1969, for uttering threats against the life of the President in violation of 18 U.S.C. § 871, and that various efforts had been made to secure evidence of crimes under investigation through the immunization of persons allegedly associated with the Black Panther Party.

On April 6, the District Court denied the motion to quash *Application of Caldwell*, 311 F.Supp. 358 (ND Cal.1970), on the ground that "every personwithin the jurisdiction of the government" is bound to testify upon being properly summoned. *Id.* at 360 (emphasis in original). Nevertheless, the court accepted respondent's First Amendment arguments to the extent of issuing a protective order providing that, although respondent had to divulge whatever information had been given to him for publication, he

> "shall not be required to reveal confidential associations, sources or information received, developed or maintained by him as a professional journalist in the course of his efforts to gather news for dissemination to the public through the press or other news media."

The court held that the First Amendment afforded respondent a privilege to refuse disclosure of such confidential information until there had been

> "a showing by the Government of a compelling and overriding national interest in requiring Mr. Caldwell's testimony which cannot be served by any alternative means." *Id.* at 362.

Subsequently,[14] the term of the grand jury expired, a new grand jury was convened, and a new subpoena ad testificandum was issued and served on May 22, 1970. A new motion to quash by respondent and memorandum in opposition by the Government were filed, and, by stipulation of the parties, the motion was submitted on the prior record. The court denied the motion to quash, repeating the protective provisions in its prior order but this time directing Caldwell to appear before the grand jury pursuant to the May 22 subpoena. Respondent refused to appear before the grand jury, and the court issued an order to show cause why he should not be held in contempt. Upon his further refusal to go before the grand jury, respondent was ordered committed for contempt until such time as he complied with the court's order or until the expiration of the term of the grand jury. Respondent Caldwell appealed the contempt order,[15] and the Court of Appeals reversed. *Caldwell v. United States*, 434 F.2d 1081 (CA9 1970). Viewing the issue before it as whether Caldwell was required to appear before the grand jury at all, rather than the scope of permissible interrogation, the court first determined that the First Amendment provided a qualified testimonial privilege to newsmen; in its view, requiring a reporter like Caldwell to testify would deter his informants from communicating with him in the future and would cause him to censor his writings in an effort to avoid being subpoenaed.

Absent compelling reasons for requiring his testimony, he was held privileged to withhold it. The court also held, for similar First Amendment reasons, that, absent some special showing of necessity by the Government, attendance by Caldwell at a secret meeting of the grand jury was something he was privileged to refuse because of the potential impact of such an appearance on the flow of news to the public. We granted the United States' petition for certiorari.[16] 402 U.S. 942 (1971).

1. What protections are available to journalists who want to ensure the protection of sources?

2. Why is it important that the press be considered trustworthy by sources?

CHAPTER 4

WHAT ADVOCACY ORGANIZATIONS SAY

Given the importance of freedom of the press, advocacy organizations around the world work to ensure journalists are able to do their jobs safely and reliably. Some groups work in countries where journalists are routinely targeted by governments to make sure international organizations are aware of violence or threats against them, while groups in countries with governments that use more subtle tactics work hard to pass legislation that protects reporters. In recent years, however, freedom of the press has been highly politicized, leading to partisan ideas of what constitutes threats to free speech. Advocacy organizations are responsible for making sure the public is aware of what threats to freedom of the press look like and how even verbal threats from those in power can have an impact on what is—and isn't—reported.

"FREEDOM OF THE PRESS," BY DEAN RUSSELL, FROM THE FOUNDATION FOR ECONOMIC EDUCATION, APRIL 1, 1965

Dr. Russell, economist, is a member of the staff of The Foundation for Economic Education.

To the best of my knowledge, freedom of the press (the printed word) is complete in the United States today. That is, anyone can still write whatever he pleases and (subject to our reasonable libel laws) the police will protect both him and his manuscript. But all too many of us confuse "freedom to write" with "what is printed." Both my liberal and conservative friends are equally guilty of this disservice to freedom. If they disagree with what is printed in the newspapers, they are often prone to complain that freedom of the press doesn't exist. That attitude demonstrates a total misunderstanding of the meaning of freedom of the press.

For example, it so happens that I am in general disagreement with the editorial viewpoints expressed by more than 90 per cent of the large daily newspapers in our country. But that fact has nothing whatever to do with the existence of freedom of the press. The only issue of consequence is whether or not the owners and editors of the newspapers are printing what they themselves choose to print—and for any good or bad reason that pleases them. If any publisher is ever compelled to print viewpoints that do not appeal to him personally, freedom of the press will be finished.

There is, of course, only one source from which that compulsion could come—government. Yet I have heard many of my teaching colleagues seriously propose the idea that newspapers should be compelled to print all viewpoints or, worse yet, that the government should establish "opposition newspapers" as a "public service." Both proposals are, of course, the reverse of freedom of the press. The only valid test of freedom of the press is this: Can you write anything you please, pay to have it printed, and send it through the mails at your own expense without police interference? If so, freedom of the press is complete. If not, there is no freedom of the press. The fact that you may not have the large amount of capital that is today required to establish a daily newspaper is in no way related to this issue.

1. According to the author, what is the test for determining the presence of a free press?

2. In your opinion, is his view of freedom of the press complete or incomplete? What else might be a factor in freedom of the press?

"OUR PRESS FREEDOM IS UNDER FIRE," BY WILLIAM A. COLLINS, FROM *OTHERWORDS*, JUNE 11, 2012

Yes, the truth
Will set us free;
But it's not found
On NBC.

Freedom of the press, that inspired rallying cry of our democracy, is becoming a poignant memory. In its latest ranking of how such freedoms stack up worldwide, Reporters Without Borders ranked the United States No. 47. We certainly rate way better than China, which clocked in at No. 174 out of 179 countries, but this truly is a shameful grade.

"The crackdown on protest movements and the accompanying excesses took their toll on journalists," the organization noted in its explanation for the nation falling by 27 places in this annual ranking. "In the space of two months in the United States, more than 25 were subjected to arrests and beatings at the hands of police who were quick to issue indictments for inappropriate behavior, public nuisance or even lack of accreditation."

The attack on media coverage of the Occupy movement's many strands continued into 2012, particularly in the police's crackdown in Oakland, California.

Meanwhile, the Pentagon has suppressed data on civilian casualties in all of our many ongoing conflicts, thus leaving the media without critical data.

Even while being stiffed by the feds for basic information, corporate newshounds too rarely raise a stink or ask embarrassing policy questions, and the major media lost interest in the Afghanistan conflict years ago. The chief cause of this government/media non-aggression pact is that the mainstream media now belongs to America's corporate family. No boat-rocking, please. The 50 corporations that controlled the vast majority of U.S. media operations in 1983, according to researcher Ben Bagdikian, seemed powerful, but by 2001, there were only seven.

In the name of consolidation, media companies of all kinds have swallowed up affiliates and subsidiaries to the point where it's almost impossible to keep track of who owns what. So while most reporters and editors get into the business to serve and protect the public interest, media managers make sure that the business serves itself. Most reporters and editors grasp this reality full well, and so tailor their product to protect their jobs.

Historically, advertising was the driving force behind this self-censorship. Today, given the declining numbers of newspaper readers and TV news junkies and the stiff competition for advertising dollars on the Internet, media outlets are scrambling for an elusive new model to pay the bills. Sure, bonanzas still crop up, such as expensive political campaigns. These aren't trends to be lightly criticized, either in print or on the air. And so they generally aren't.

But what about public radio and TV programming? Didn't the government encourage public broadcasting in large part to ensure that audiences would be offered alternative views? Well maybe, but often that's not the case. And while PBS and NPR remain dependent on Congress for their legal existence, government spending accounts for only a small portionof their overall budgets. Worse, our "public" radio and TV stations run corporate ads that acknowledge donations that keep them on the air. All those oil company greenwashing commercials make it sound like they only traffic in granola and solar panels.

Today's top media battles, however, increasingly involve the Internet. Corporate service providers are fighting mightily to have it serve corporate interests, while media reform organizations are striving desperately for journalistic freedom. Worst of all, censorship is gaining ground, especially when it's disguised as "cybersecurity" measures.

1. What does it mean that the United States is ranked the way it is by Reporters Without Borders?

2. According to the author, what are some challenges to freedom of the press today?

"COALITION CALLS FOR RELEASE OF MEXICAN JOURNALIST SEEKING POLITICAL ASYLUM IN US," BY DIEGO MENDOZA-MOYERS, FROM *CRONKITE NEWS*, APRIL 06, 2017

PHOENIX — As attacks against reporters in Mexico increase, a coalition of immigration lawyers and organizations that defend journalists are calling for the release of a Mexican reporter detained at the border after asking for political asylum in the United States.

Paris-based Reporters Without Borders is urging the U.S. government to release Martin Mendez Piñeda, a reporter fleeing Acapulco, Guerrero in southern Mexico.

"This journalist, who has been persecuted and threatened with death in his country, must be allowed to present his case for political asylum freely and with dignity before an immigration judge," Emmanuel Colombié, the head of Reporters With Borders' Latin America bureau, said in a statement issued by the organization.

Martin Mendez Pineda is being held an Immigration Customs Enforcement detention center in El Paso. He was taken into custody February 5th after requesting political asylum at an international bridge.

Mendez worked for Novedades Acapulco, where he said he faced death threats and federal police officers beat him for coverage of what he described as violent arrests carried out by police at the scene of a road accident last year.

"Because of the Mexican Federal officers' and Mexican Military's ability to locate Mr. Mendez anywhere within the country, he is in imminent danger," Carlos Spector, an immigration lawyer in El Paso representing Mendez said in a letter to ICE authorities. "He has no other option but to come to the United States to seek political asylum."

Mendez passed a "credible fear" interview, a key step to determine whether an asylum applicant's case moves forward, according to Spector, who specializes in political asylum cases. He said Mendez is asking to be released from detention on parole until an immigration judge decides his case. He said he will stay with his cousin, a U.S. citizen living in California.

ICE notified Mendez they would not grant him parole, citing concerns that Mendez "did not establish, to ICE's satisfaction, substantial ties to the community" and would be a flight risk. "Imposition of a bond or other condition of parole would not ensure, to ICE's satisfaction, your appearance at required immigration hearings pending the outcome of your case," ICE authorities said in a notice sent to Mendez.

ICE officials declined to comment on the specific decision but in a statement said, "Parole determinations by U.S. Immigration and Customs Enforcement are made on a case-by-case basis, taking into account all aspects of the case, including safety considerations and any sensitivities involving the case."

Menedez's lawyer said President Donald Trump's executive orders on immigration have led to "a blanket denial of parole" for asylum seekers.

"And so, as a result of that, we have come to learn that while, 40 to 50 percent of asylum seekers used to be granted access after passing credible fear... now its zero," said Spector.

March has been a particularly bloody month for journalists in Mexico. Three reporters were murdered, the most recent Miroslava Breach, a 54-year-old reporter for the *La Jornada*, was gunned down in Chihuahua City March 23rd.

She was also a contributor for *El Norte in Ciudad Juarez*. The editor of the newspaper has since announced it will shut down, citing safety concerns. In a front-page article with the headline "Adios," editor Oscar Cantu Murgia said he "is not willing to pay with one more life of my collaborators, or my own."

The Committee to Protect Journalists counts 92 journalists and media workers who have been killed in Mexico since 1992, 38 of those murders have been confirmed as being directly linked to the journalists' work with a majority of the cases unsolved.

"In terms of the justice system, impunity is kind of a norm," Carlos Lauria, CPJ Americas program director, said. "One of the issues that we have seen is that this problem is going way beyond the press. It's not just a problem for freedom only, it has become a serious freedom of expression crisis, in the sense that fundamental human rights are being affected by the violence."

CPJ and Reporters Without Borders both cite Mexico as the most dangerous country in the western hemisphere for journalists, though measures of how many journalists have been murdered as a result of their work varies.

According to Reporters Without Borders, a record number of 11 journalists were killed in 2016.

Mexico is ranked 149th out of 180 countries in Reporters Without Borders' World Press Freedom Index, which measures the degree of freedom available to journalists in a specific nation.

"Mexico is one of the most dangerous countries for the press in the world. Deadliest in the western hemisphere," said Carlos Lauria, CPJ Americas program director "Many Mexicans and journalists are not able to exercise freely their freedom of expression because there's this climate of fear and intimidation that it's basically inhibiting the press from fulfilling its role…It is damaging the quality of the democratic system, no question about that."

1. Why is the Mexican government targeting this journalist?

2. Do countries like the United States have an obligation to protect journalists from other countries?

"IN US AND WORLDWIDE, STUDY SHOWS 'NEVER A MORE DANGEROUS TIME TO BE A JOURNALIST'," BY JULIA CONLEY, FROM *COMMON DREAMS*, NOVEMBER 30, 2017

A new report finds that threats to global journalistic freedoms are at an all-time high, with attacks on the press being increasingly reported in democratic countries as well as under authoritarian regimes.

The freedom of expression advocacy group Article 19 and online database V-Dem compiled data from 172 countries between 2006 and 2016, rating each based on their levels of internet censorship, harassment and intimidation of journalists, media bias and corruption, and other indicators.

Turkey, Egypt, Burundi, and Venezuela, all of which have experienced political crises in recent years and whose human rights abuses have been addressed by the U.S., each saw large declines in press freedom over the last decade, according to the study.

But President Donald Trump's attacks on the media and the spread of information did not go unnoticed by the researchers, who placed the president in the same category as leaders who have been accused for years of authoritarianism.

It seems likely that the growing trend of 'strong men' leaders like Trump, Putin, Duterte, and Erdoğan, who have little concern about public oversight and accountability, will reduce the amount of information available about their activities even in countries with effective legislation. Already, there has been systematic elimination of information on U.S. government websites about issues such as climate change.

In an interview with the *Guardian* on Thursday, Robert Mahoney of the Committee to Protect Journalists, said that there was "never been a more dangerous time to be a journalist," including in the U.S.

"The United States has traditionally been a beacon of press freedom and defender of journalists but a barrage of anti-press rhetoric from President Trump undermines the role of the press in a democracy and potentially endangers journalists," said Mahoney. "Labeling reporting you don't like as 'fake news' sends a signal to authoritarian leaders globally that it's okay to crack down on the press."

The report also expressed grave concerns about Britain's Investigatory Powers Act of 2016, which Article 19 called "one of the most draconian surveillance legislation of any democracy, offering a template for authoritarian regimes and seriously undermining the rights of its citizens to privacy and freedom of expression."

More than 250 journalists worldwide were imprisoned last year, while 79 were killed. Countries where journalists' safety is considered to be the most threatened include Honduras, Mexico, and the Philippines, where reporters cover those countries' drug wars, and Turkey, where journalists who cover opposing views to the Erdogan regime are intimidated and detained. On social media, many drew attention to the report, particularly noting that democratic countries were far from exempt from Article 19's findings.

1. According to this article, why is it a particularly dangerous time to be a journalist today?

2. What can be done to curb these dangers?

CHAPTER 5

WHAT THE MEDIA SAY

How does the press report on its own role, and in what ways do threats to freedom of the press register in the media? In recent years the media has adapted to ensure reporting on threats to their own work, including writing about trends from outside the federal government that might become challenges to press freedom in years to come. As the internet has grown, so too has the way the press interacts with the public, challenging conventional ideas of what constitutes the press and how they should fulfill their obligation to the public. Even as the internet has made it possible to access news and reporting from around the world, governments have found ways to curtail its usage while the proliferation of sites have given rise to concerns about what can and cannot be considered legitimate media sources that are protected by constitutional law.

"DOES BILLIONAIRE-FUNDED LAWSUIT AGAINST GAWKER CREATE PLAYBOOK FOR PUNISHING MEDIA?," BY CLAY CALVERT, FROM *THE CONVERSATION*, MAY 29, 2016

Word last week that Silicon Valley billionaire Peter Thiel bankrolled wrestler Hulk Hogan's invasion-of-privacy lawsuit against Gawker added a wrinkle to a case already featuring colorful characters and a US$140 million jury verdict.

At a sensational and personal level, the story highlights the animus between PayPal co-founder Thiel and Gawker founder Nick Denton stemming from a 2007 gossip item that publicly outed Thiel as gay. Thiel sees Denton as "a singularly terrible bully" who invades privacy for profit. In turn, Denton sympathetically portrays Gawker, in an open letter to Thiel, as "a small New York media company" being bullied by a man with "a net worth of more than $2 billion."

But regardless of whether it's framed as a personal battle between Thiel and Denton or a larger one between protecting privacy and a free press, the revelation raises important questions about third-party financed litigation targeting U.S. news media outlets that are safeguarded under the First Amendment.

Most importantly, should third-party-funded litigation against news organizations be banned by lawmakers? This is the kind of issue I explore at the Marion B. Brechner First Amendment Project at the University of Florida, which

I've directed for the past six years, and in my book about privacy and articles about various threats to a free press.

THREATS TO A FREE PRESS

The fear from First Amendment advocates in the press advocates is palpable. They see Thiel as creating a playbook for other billionaires and millionaires to take on and silence members of the news media. As Vox correspondent Timothy B. Lee writes:

> *The threat to freedom of the press is obvious. Any news organization doing its job is going to make some enemies. If a wealthy third party is willing to bankroll lawsuits by anyone with a grudge, and defending each case costs millions of dollars, the organization could get driven out of business even if it wins every single lawsuit.*

Others agree that Thiel has "created a model where any thin-skinned billionaire can ruin a media company without even telling anyone."

In other words, billionaires who feel they have been libeled or had their privacy invaded by a news organization can score legal victories against the press via third-party funding of lawsuits in one of two different ways.

First, the sheer fear of such lawsuits may result in self-censorship by news organizations who choose not to criticize a wealthy individual rather than risk fighting a potentially expensive and protracted legal battle.

Second, even if such a chilling effect does not occur and a critical story actually is published, the costs of defending a lawsuit arising from it can be enormous.

LEVELING THE PLAYING FIELD

Indeed, Thiel has been villainized in some media quarters for his "cloak-and-dagger tactics" and satirized in others since it was discovered he funded Hogan's lawsuit.

Denton blasts Thiel as someone who, "despite all the success and public recognition that a person could dream of, seethes over criticism and plots behind the scenes to tie up his opponents in litigation he can afford better than they."

But has Thiel broken any laws? Apparently not. Professor Eugene Kontorovich of Northwestern University, for example, emphasizes that what Thiel did "is well within the parameters of third-party involvement in lawsuits."

In fact, some scholars contend that third-party financing of plaintiff lawsuits actually represents "another step in leveling the playing field between plaintiffs and defendants."

Why might that be true in a libel or privacy case against the news media? Because most plaintiffs' attorneys in such cases work on a contingency fee basis. That puts plaintiffs at a disadvantage because it means their lawyers collect money down the road only if they win – aside from, perhaps, a modest retainer upfront to cover the initial costs of getting the case going.

Rather than billing clients by the hour, as media defense attorneys do, plaintiffs' attorneys in libel and privacy cases thus take a large financial risk that they may not collect any money if they lose. This, in turn, may make them less likely to take such a case in the first place.

NOBILITY OF PURPOSE?

The practice of champerty, in which a person or company steps in to help fund a case in return for a cut of the potential payoff, thus allows some lawsuits to go forward that otherwise might not because an attorney doesn't want to take on the cost or the risk of not recovering anything.

Thiel's lawsuit distorts this concept because he does not seek money but rather has a personal motive. Thus, at least one major litigation funding firm, Burford Capital, has distanced itself from the current fracas. As CEO Chris Bogart notes in a blog posting:

> *What Burford and other commercial litigation financiers do is part of a large and pretty boring business around commercial litigation – businesses suing each other... That world is miles away from professional wrestling, sex tapes and "revenge litigation." We don't have anything to do with that other, more salacious world.*

Third-party litigation funding by the likes of Burford Capital is far from rare today and, in fact, "is prevalent in litigation and arbitration both domestically and internationally."

Had, however, Thiel been funding a lawsuit for a more noble cause – one not for revenge against an entity that is part of the media – we might see it differently. As First Amendment defense attorney Marc Randazza observes:

> *When the ACLU represents a party in an important civil rights case, isn't that a third party funding a case to promote an agenda? What about the NRA? It happens all the time.*

Northwestern's Kontorovich concurs, noting that "anyone who donates to the ACLU or a Legal Aid fund is basically underwriting third-party litigation."

For Thiel's part, he emphasizes that his motives are "less about revenge and more about specific deterrence."

> I saw Gawker pioneer a unique and incredibly damaging way of getting attention by bullying people even when there was no connection with the public interest... I thought it was worth fighting back.

THE REAL DANGER

In any case, is the sky now suddenly going to fall on the mainstream news media? Are the odds in favor of Thiel or others like him striking a future $140 million jackpot against a media defendant?

It is highly doubtful. As Slate's Mark Joseph Stern points out, Thiel essentially:

> lucked out with Hogan's judge and jury — it's hard to imagine a court more sympathetic to Hogan's claims — but there's no reason to think future plaintiffs will be so wildly fortunate. Yes, deep-pocketed donors could theoretically finance frivolous yet costly nuisance lawsuits and pester publications into oblivion. But most such suits would be dismissed early on, and an attorney who brings overtly frivolous claims risks court sanction. In short, it is exceedingly rare for the stars to align as neatly as they did for Hogan.

Yet, even if a media defendant ultimately prevails in court against a third-party financed lawsuit, it still has rung up potentially massive bills to pay its attorneys and other costs in fighting that battle. That is the real danger here.

Ultimately, however, the First Amendment protects the press against government censorship, not private third-party funding of lawsuits that target it. If change is to occur, then, because of the fear of another billionaire running the Thiel playbook against a media organization, it will take legislation.

A first baby step, as it were, for such legislation might concentrate on transparency. It would

require attorneys who accept third-party funding for cases to file documents in public court files related to those cases to acknowledge and identify all sources of funding beyond those coming directly from clients.

Completely banning the practice of third-party litigation seems impractical, however, given both how well instantiated it now is in the U.S. and that it can support legitimate plaintiffs who might not otherwise possess the fiscal resources to do battle in court. But openness, regarding who funds whom, will make the public aware about the individuals or businesses that hold a vested monetary stake or, in Thiel's case, a non-pecuniary one, in the outcome.

Indeed, it seems to be the secretiveness of Thiel's funding that has so many taken aback.

1. According to the author, what implications could the Gawker lawsuit have for freedom of the press?

2. What are some ways that public opinion and the press can be balanced?

"DANGER TO A FREE PRESS," BY JOHN C. MERRILL, FROM THE FOUNDATION FOR ECONOMIC EDUCATION, JUNE 1, 1965

Dr. Merrill, Associate Professor of Journalism at the University of Missouri, offers, among others, a graduate course on "Basic Issues in the News."

Although isolated journalists, statesmen, and academicians had long toyed with the term "responsibility" as well as "freedom" for the mass media, it was not until 1947 when the Commission on Freedom of the Press (headed by Robert Hutchins) brought out its *A Free and Responsible Press* that the concept gained much of an ideological foothold in the United States. Earlier, it had somehow been assumed that responsibility was automatically built into a libertarian press; that a "free press" in the Western sense was responsible per se to its society.

But the Hutchins group thought differently. Noting what they called a clear danger in growing restriction of communications outlets and general irresponsibility in many areas of the press, the group offered this ominous warning: "If they (the agencies of mass communication) are irresponsible, not even the First Amendment will protect their freedom from governmental control. The amendment will be amended."

Since 1947 there has been growing discourse about the responsibility of the press and less and less about its freedom to react independently in a democratic society. Undoubtedly many would-be "definers" of responsible journalism are among us who are ready and willing to turn our press in a new direction: toward "consensus" journalism hewing to some predetermined line which the "responsibility" proponents see as progress.

WHAT IS "SOCIAL RESPONSIBILITY"?

At first it would seem rather strange that modern liberals are in the forefront of the "social responsibility" advocates and thus opposed to our traditional pluralistic press philosophy. However, when one thinks of their skepticism as to the value of the individual, it is not too difficult to see them projecting this rationale to the press. Just as "liberals" are opposed to "laissez faire" economics, they are also opposed to "laissez faire" journalism. Inevitably, if they have their way, the American press can expect a great amount of control in the name of "responsible journalism" and a minimum of individual publisher freedom.

The social responsibility "theory" implies a recognition by the media that they must perform a public service to warrant their existence. Facts must be reported accurately and in a meaningful context. Responsibility, instead of freedom, must be the watchword. Such thinking leads to the advocacy of a regulatory system designed to keep the press "socially responsible."

This so-called theory of social responsibility, seriously embraced in "liberal" circles, has a good ring to it and, like "love" and "motherhood," has an undeniable attraction for many. There is a trend throughout the world in this direction, which implies a suspicion of, and dissatisfaction with, the libertarianism of Milton, Locke, and even Jefferson. Implicit in this trend toward "social responsibility" is the argument that some group (obviously a governmental one, ultimately) can and must define or decide just what is socially responsible. Also, the implication is clear that publishers and journalists acting freely cannot determine what is socially responsible nearly as well as can some "outside" or "impartial" group. If this power elite decides that the press (or portions of it) is not responsible, not even the First Amendment will keep publishers from losing their freedom.

This would appear to many as a suggestion of increased power accumulation at the national level, a further restriction of a pluralistic society.

GOVERNMENT SUPERVISION

Few would deny that the press, in one respect, would be more "responsible» if some type of governmental supervision came about; indeed, reporters could be kept from nosing about in "critical" areas during "critical" times. The amount of sensational material could be controlled in the press, or eliminated altogether. Government activities could always be supported and public policy could be pushed regularly. The press could be more "educational" in the sense that less hard news (crime, wrecks, disasters, and the like) would appear, while more news of art exhibits, concerts, speeches by government personages, and national progress in general could be emphasized. In short, the press would stress the positive and eliminate, or minimize, the negative. Then, with one voice, the press of the nation would be responsible to its society; and the definition of "responsible" would be functional—defined and carried out by the government.

Some persons may object to this line of analysis, saying that to guarantee "social responsibility" of the press does not necessarily imply government control. It is not difficult, however, to project control ultimately to government, since if left to be defined by various publishers or journalistic groups the term "social responsibility" is relative and nebulous. It is obvious that in the traditional context of American libertarianism no "solution" that would be widely agreed upon or enforced could ever be reached by nongovernment groups or individuals.

Social responsibility proponents insist that government would intervene "only when the need is great and the stakes are high." They assure us that the government should not be heavy-handed. The question arises, however, as to just when is the need great enough and the stakes high enough for government to intervene. And just how much intervention by government is enough to be "heavy-handed"?

"SOCIAL RESPONSIBILITY" IMPLIES PLURALISTIC COMMUNICATION

The American press has been proceeding on unregulated initiative up until now. But its "liberal" critics do not think that a pluralistic information system is good enough. Under the diversified system we now have—including much nonconformist journalism—the citizen does get information and a wealth of it. Admittedly, there are gaps in it, but anyone vaguely familiar with information theory and semantics knows that there will always be gaps, and if different reporters observe and communicate it, there will always be variant versions.

It is certainly not contended here that all information coming to the public from all mass media is reliable, honest, complete, fair, and "socially responsible" (whatever that means). Nobody really knows just how much of it is—or if any of it is. Since, in a nation such as the United States, there is no ready definition for "social responsibility," there is really no standard to which our media seek to conform— even though, without a doubt, they would all conceive of themselves as "socially responsible."

Their very pluralism—their very diversity—is the base of their nebulous idea that in our society they are responsible. Responsibility to our society implies a continuance of this very pluralistic communication, with all of its virtues and evils, and a constant guard against any encroachments by any group on any level to "define" what is "responsible," thereby further aligning the press to its definition.

This "press pluralism" concept seems much sounder and certainly more meaningful, than "social responsibility." All press systems can claim to be responsible to their societies, but the idea of a pluralistic media system injecting a variety of opinions and ideas into the social fabric is one which only the libertarian system can reasonably claim. The U.S. press should fight all attempts to cast all of its units in the same mold; the right of, or at least the possibility for, some press units to deviate from others must persist. If that be irresponsibility, we had better be content to continue living with it.

1. According to the author, what threats did he see to freedom of the press in 1965?

2. Given what you've learned so far, compare and contrast the author's views on press freedom with those we see today.

"THE VIRGINIA ON-AIR SHOOTINGS: ALL TOO REAL," BY RUSSELL FRANK, FROM *THE CONVERSATION*, APRIL 16, 2015

In an interview with the *New York Times Sunday Book Review* this week, children's author R.L. Stine joked that he never reads nonfiction: "I hate anything real."

Stine could have been speaking for the legion of commentators who spoke out about the on-camera shooting of two journalists and an interviewee in Virginia on Wednesday. But apparently, he wouldn't be speaking for many people in the media.

Fictional on-screen killings are as common as weather reports. Real ones are rare: Jack Ruby's killing of Lee Harvey Oswald two days after Oswald shot President Kennedy and a suicide on a Los Angeles freeway in 1998 are among the few that viewers could see as they happened.

In such unfolding situations, TV station managers can argue that they had no way of knowing that the incident would end the way it did and could not cut away in time. The real controversy centers on re-broadcast of the ghastly footage. Here, the suicide of Pennsylvania State Treasurer Budd Dwyer in 1987 enters the picture.

WHAT TO SHOW

It was the day before Dwyer's sentencing on fraud charges. He called a news conference in Harrisburg and after reading a statement, with cameras rolling, he put a gun in his mouth and fired.

Most Pennsylvania TV stations got the footage around a half-hour later. Most only showed Dwyer brandishing the gun. A couple showed him putting the gun in his mouth, but cut away before he pulled the trigger. Three showed him pulling the trigger.

A similar range of decisions was on display within the first few hours of the shooting of journalists Alison Parker and Adam Ward and local official Vicki Gardner in Moneta, Virginia.

At first, NBC News froze the video before the shooting started. "We're not going to show you the entire sequence," the anchor said. Later, though, the network posted a warning that the video "may be disturbing to some viewers," then ran the entire clip.

CBS News warned viewers orally that the footage would be disturbing, then showed it.

ABC froze the video at the moment when Parker appeared to have been shot – perhaps the least palatable approach. Not surprisingly, WDBJ-TV, the station Parker and Shaw worked for, shied away.

"We are choosing not to run the video of that right now," station manager Jeff Marks said, "because frankly, we don't need to see it again, and our staff doesn't need to see it again."

Which raises the fundamental question about such video: Does anybody need to see it?

Unlike the mainstream news organizations, social media managers decided that the answer was no: While the broadcast and cable giants showed the interview footage shot by Adam Ward for WDBJ, Facebook and Twitter took down the images recorded by shooter Vester Lee Flanagan on his cell phone.

MEDIA AND COPYCATS

The question of how we are harmed by viewing real as opposed to staged violence is the main ethics issue raised by coverage of the shootings in Virginia, but there are others. One is the attention paid to the perpetrator.

During the spate of school shootings in the late 1990s, there was much discussion of whether news coverage of each incident spawned copycats. If, the thinking went, these shooters were motivated, in part, by the desire to see their faces and their words on the front pages of newspapers and in the lead stories on the evening news, perhaps news organizations would do better to ignore them and focus on the victims.

Yet, as ever, we are seeing multiple images of Flanagan, including a dramatic, if blurry shot of him firing his gun, and even a quote from a letter in which he expressed his admiration for the shooters at Columbine High School and Virginia Tech University.

As the afternoon wore on, ABC's homepage led with "What we know about suspect in on-air shooting" and NBC's with "Human Powder Keg: Gunman Says Discrimination."

Certainly we humans have always been fascinated with the criminal mind — with what makes transgressors tick. But is the possible role of the news media in inspiring copycat criminals even part of the newsroom discussion anymore?

FALSE FRAMING

A third familiar issue raised by the coverage is the over-hastiness to report what has not yet been confirmed. As we saw with the coverage of the wounding of White House Press Secretary James Brady during the attempted assassination of President Reagan in 1981, and with the wounding of Representative Gabrielle Giffords in 2011, some outlets were reporting Flanagan's death while others were telling us that he was in critical condition or that he "still had a pulse."

Reporters were also quick to frame the story as part of a growing pattern of violence against journalists, but since the shooter turned out to be a journalist himself, this appears to be a case of a "disgruntled former employee" who just happened to be a journalist.

Finally, it is worth noting that in headline after headline, the incident is referred to as an "on-air" shooting. Clearly, the fact that this crime was committed as the camera rolled vastly increased its newsworthiness.

Horrified as we are, or claim to be, by real violence, televised real violence that we can watch as it unfolds is realer than real and, therefore, vastly more fascinating than the kind we find out about after the fact.

Or so the mainstream news media believes.

1. How do incidents like the shooting in Virginia impact reporting?

2. Does this shooting constitute a potential threat to press freedom?

"DEADLY WORDS: THE SPIKE IN KILLINGS OF MEXICAN JOURNALISTS," BY GUILIA MCDONNELL NIETO DEL RIO, FROM *FOREIGN POLICY IN FOCUS*, JULY 6, 2017

"Let them kill us all, if that is the death sentence for reporting this hell. No to silence."

That was Mexican journalist Javier Valdez's defiant reaction to the brutal killing of his journalist colleague Miroslava Breach, who was gunned down in the state of Chihuahua, Mexico this spring.

Less than two months later, on May 15th, Valdez himself was shot and killed in the streets of Culiacán, capital of the northern state of Sinaloa. The state is home to the powerful Sinaloa Cartel, long headed by the legendary Joaquin "El Chapo" Guzman, now jailed in New York awaiting trial on U.S. charges.

Valdez is the sixth journalist killed in Mexico just this year. According to Reporters Without Borders, Mexico is now the third most dangerous country for reporting, just after Syria and Afghanistan. Shortly before Valdez's murder, *The New York Times* reported that since 2000, at least 104 journalists have been killed in Mexico, while another 25 remain disappeared.

Although almost all of the journalists attacked in recent years have been Mexican nationals, the escalation of killings raises questions about the safety of all media workers in Mexico.

Several high-profile journalists have been killed and wounded in conflict zones like Syria, Iraq, and Libya in the past couple of years, but Mexico features a different kind of conflict — less about artillery and aerial bombing, which kill indiscriminately, and more about targeted individuals being "disappeared" or subject to assassination. Still, the death toll in Mexico approaches war-like heights.

A CLIMATE OF IMPUNITY

In many cases, human rights advocates say, the journalists targeted were investigating links between criminal syndicates, local politicians, and law enforcement authorities. The sinister connections between government and criminal groups with access to vast amounts of cash has long plagued Mexico and undermined democracy south of the border.

In 2011, Valdez received the International Press Freedom Award from the Committee to Protect Journalists in New York. The prestigious award honors journalists who have done commendable work across the globe. And if a figure as well-known and respected internationally as Javier Valdez could be targeted, it seems, so could any journalist working in Mexico.

Of course, journalists are only a minority of those affected by crime in Mexico. Since 2006, more than 80,000 people have been lost due to violence in the country, according to a 2015 Congressional Research Service report. The situation will only worsen if journalists investigating and reporting on these crimes are silenced.

Human rights groups, such as the Committee to Protect Journalists, have for years been calling on the Mexican government to punish those responsible for the violence. According to a recent article published in *The Intercept*, the Mexican government's human rights commission reported that in 2016, 90 percent of crimes against journalists were either unsolved or the perpetrators faced no consequences.

WASHINGTON ADDS FUEL TO THE FIRE

Meanwhile, the U.S. may be making the problem worse. Washington, after all, is funding the Mexican government's failing fight against drugs — regardless of the extremely high levels of corruption in Mexico's security institutions. Often the very policemen investigating these crimes against journalists are involved with the drug cartels themselves.

In June, *The New York Times* reported that the Mexican government has been using spyware to retrieve private information from human rights lawyers, anti-corruption figures, and journalists through their smartphones — information that some worry could be used to track and target human rights defenders.

But Washington continues to send semi-automatic weapons, helicopters, and armored vehicles, among other amenities to a government in which some sectors appear implicated in an effort to silence the free press. Under a program called the Mérida Initiative, the U.S. has sent more than $2.6 billion worth of this assistance to Mexico, in many cases funding corrupt officials who are often involved in violence against the very people they're meant to protect.

Adding to the chaotic situation, illegal gun trafficking across the U.S.-Mexico border has supplied both drug cartels and police officials with weaponry to continue human rights abuses.

"A FIELD STREWN WITH EXPLOSIVES"

Unfortunately, not enough is being done to find justice for the lives of so many great journalists lost. Both the U.S. and Mexican governments should be doing more to ensure that journalists' lives, like those of others, are protected in this violent and lengthy conflict.

The murder of Valdez, a man working tirelessly to expose the inner abuses of drug cartels in Sinaloa, is a tremendous loss for the international human rights community.

Valdez was known for lending a hand to U.S. and other journalists who arrived in Sinaloa to write about Mexico's drug wars. He was always generous with his time, according to many in the international and Mexican journalist community. At the end of the day, however, the foreign journalists went home. Valdez stayed in Sinaloa, vulnerable to the crime bosses and crooked politicians.

In 2011, Valdez's acceptance speech for the International Press Freedom Award reflected the unparalleled dangers of working as a journalist in Mexico.

"Where I work, Culiacán, in the state of Sinaloa, Mexico, it is dangerous to be alive, and to do journalism is to walk on an invisible line drawn by the bad guys — who are in drug trafficking and in the government — in a field strewn with explosives," he said. "This is what most of the country is living through. We, the citizens, are providing the deaths, and the Mexican and U.S. governments, the guns."

His words still resound today and every day. It's up to both Washington and Mexico to ensure that Valdez — and human rights defenders like him — doesn't become just another number in the casualty count.

1. How can the international community ensure freedom of the press?

2. How can reporters who work in conflict zones be protected? Is ensuring their safety part of freedom of the press? Why or why not?

CHAPTER 6

WHAT ORDINARY PEOPLE SAY

The role of the press is ultimately to inform the public, allowing them to make decisions regarding the governing of their country in addition to other important issues that impact their nation. Curtailing freedom of the press inhibits the ability of reporters and journalists to do this important work, which can have wide-ranging consequences for the electorate and for the country. But partisanship can influence what the public considers fair, truthful, or worthwhile reporting, and many have recently called for greater stringency in monitoring what is considered journalism. As we've learned, business and government sometimes have less than the best interests of the press in mind when they try to limit access or otherwise obstruct reporting, making it the public's duty to remain watchful for possible infringement that will shape the way they see their world.

"THESE LAWS MAKE ME WANT TO GAG," BY WILL POTTER, FROM *OTHERWORDS*, FEBRUARY 20, 2013

Do you have a right to know where that steak on your plate came from?

Should it be legal to photograph chicken farms and dairy cows?

Big Agriculture says you don't and it shouldn't. Armies of Big Ag lobbyists are pushing for new state-level laws across the country to keep us all in the dark. Less restrictive versions have been law in some states since the 1980s, but the meat industry has ratcheted up a radical new campaign.

This wave of "ag-gag" bills would criminalize whistleblowers, investigators, and journalists who expose animal welfare abuses at factory farms and slaughterhouses. Ten states considered "ag-gag" bills last year, and Iowa, Missouri, and Utah approved them. Even more are soon to follow.

Had these laws been in force, the Humane Society might have been prosecuted for documenting repeated animal welfare and food safety violations at Hallmark/Westland, formerly the second-largest supplier of beef to the National School Lunch Program. Cows too sick to walk were being slaughtered and that meat was shipped to our schools, endangering our kids. The investigation led to the largest meat recall in U.S. history.

More recently in Wyoming, video footage showed workers at a Tyson supplier kicking live piglets and pummeling mother pigs. The film led to criminal charges against nine employees, including two managers. In Pennsylvania, an investigation of a major regional egg supplier, Kreider Farms, showed decomposing birds packed into cages among the living. Other hens had their heads stuck in cage wire and were left to die.

Big Ag wants to silence whistleblowers rather than clean up its act. Ag-gag bills are now pending in Pennsylvania, Arkansas, Indiana, Nebraska, and New Hampshire. Similar legislation may crop up in North Carolina and Minnesota.

The bills aren't identical, but they share common language — sometimes even word-for-word. Some criminalize anyone who even "records an image or sound" from a factory farm. Others mandate that witnesses report abuses within a few hours, which would make it impossible for whistleblowers to secure advice and protection, or for them to document a pattern of abuses.

Indiana's version of this cookie-cutter legislation ominously begins with the statement that farmers have the right to "engage in agricultural operations free from the threat of terrorism and interference from unauthorized third persons."

Yet these bills aren't about violence or terrorism. They're about truth-telling that's bad for branding. For these corporations, a "terrorist" is anyone who threatens their profits by exposing inhumane practices that jeopardize consumer health.

It's too early to tell how many of these bills stand a chance of passing. But ag-gag supporters have no shortage of wealth and political influence.

As a journalist, I'm worried about what these bills mean for freedom of the press. And the investigators and whistleblowers I have interviewed are deeply concerned about their own safety and freedom.

Ag-gag bills aren't about silencing journalists and whistleblowers. They're about curbing consumer access to information at a time when more and more Americans want to know where our food comes from and how it's produced.

The problem for corporations is that when people have information, they act on it. During a recent ag-gag hearing in Indiana, one of the nation's largest egg producers told lawmakers about a recent investigation. After an undercover video was posted online, 50 customers quickly called and stopped buying their eggs. An informed public is the biggest threat to business as usual.

An informed public is also the biggest threat to these ag-gag bills. In Wyoming, one of the bills has already failed. According to sponsors, it was abandoned in part because of negative publicity. By shining a light on these attempts, we can make sure that the rest fail as well, while protecting the right of consumers to know what they're buying.

1. What are "ag-gag bills" and how do they influence reporting?

2. When reporting on businesses and privately owned organizations, is there a right to press access?

"NO HAPPY ENDING IN HONDURAS," BY EMILY SCHWARTZ GRECO, FROM *OTHERWORDS*, FEBRUARY 20, 2010

Did you know the Atlantic coast of Honduras features miles of stunning undeveloped beaches frequented only by local villagers? Or that its Mayan ruins at Copán are as haunting and spectacular as what you'd find in Guatemala or southern Mexico?

Maybe that sounds enticing, but Honduras isn't drawing the waves of tourists Costa Rica has lured. And that's not just because its food is lackluster. Honduras is experiencing the worst political turmoil in Latin America—thanks in part to the Obama administration's embrace of a regrettable U.S. foreign policy tradition.

This tradition involves making a fuss about democratic processes when Latin American leaders attempt to help the impoverished majority, empathizing with arch-conservatives when they oust those leaders, pretending the ensuing elections staged by the arch-conservatives are "free and fair," and ignoring the bloody aftermath.

Here's a snapshot of Honduras' astounding recent history:

- June 28, 2009: Masked soldiers drag Honduran President Manuel Zelaya into a plane headed out of the country. In his pajamas. Months of dramatic mobilization and repression ensue, during which Zelaya manages to sneak back and hole up for weeks in the Brazilian embassy in Tegucigalpa.

- Nov. 29, 2009: Porfirio Lobo wins elections boycotted by Zelaya's supporters and shunned by observers from the European Union and the Organization of American States (OAS), which expelled Honduras from its organization after the coup.
- Jan. 28, 2010: Lobo is sworn in.
- July 29, 2010: Human Rights Watch issues a report decrying the rampant murders of Honduran journalists and other abuses in the first six months of Lobo's government.

In one of the report's damning examples, José Oswaldo Martínez, a journalist with Radio Uno in San Pedro Sula, said he "had received repeated death threats in phone calls, text messages, and emails, including one in July that said: 'Because you won't stop talking about that dog Zelaya, we are going to shut your mouth with a bullet.'"

Things are just getting worse. In August, the National Autonomous University of Honduras "turned into a battlefield between students and repressive forces, who beat, gassed, tortured and captured students at the request of university authorities," according to the Committee of Families of the Detained and Disappeared of Honduras, known as COFADEH. The university "has become a military and police state," writes Juan Almendares, its former rector.

In addition to the eight journalists killed in the first six months after Lobo was sworn in, several more have since died or suffered savage beatings, according to COFADEH, which has joined several organizations to form a coalition called the Human Rights Platform of Honduras. Almendares and other representatives of this coalition will come to Washington in October to receive the Letelier-Moffitt international award at an annual ceremony where my organization, the Institute for Policy Studies, celebrates human rights heroes.

Despite the horrors that have taken place in Honduras, Secretary of State Hillary Clinton insists that Lobo's election was "free and fair," and demands that the Organization of American States let the country rejoin that democracies-only club.

Her callous response won't work in light of Latin America's recent transformation. In the dark days when dictators ruled much of Latin America, the OAS wouldn't have made any fuss. Today, however, the region's democracies are thriving. Most of their economies have also diversified and become far less dependent on the United States as an export market. They're standing up for Honduras because that's what they'd expect their neighbors to do if the same thing happened in their country.

And Hondurans are also standing up for themselves. The Human Rights Platform of Honduras established an independent Truth Commission to investigate human rights violations that have occurred since the coup. Exposing the truth about the brutality going on in Honduras, coupled with courageous street heat, may go a long way toward halting this madness.

1. Why would the Honduran government target journalists?

2. What does the response to this violence from Latin American countries show about the role of the international community in preserving press freedom?

"I AM AN ENEMY OF THE PEOPLE," BY JOHN FEFFER, FROM *FOREIGN POLICY IN FOCUS*, MARCH 15, 2017

Even before the election of Donald Trump — and his extraordinary declaration that the media are the "enemies of the people" — U.S. journalism was in trouble.

According to Gallup polling, American trust in mass media plummeted from an already low 40 percent in 2015 to a historic low of 32 percent in September 2016. The drop in the trust that Republicans have in the media was staggering: from 32 percent to a mere 14 percent. This last number applies as well to Trump supporters regardless of party affiliation.

If I were a Trump supporter, I'd probably look askance at the mainstream media as well. First of all, newspapers overwhelmingly backed Hillary Clinton for president: 240 editorial boards supported Clinton while only 19 favored Trump.

It wasn't so much that editorial boards are generally liberal. In 2012, after all, Mitt Romney received 105 endorsements, while Barack Obama got only 99. Rather, regardless of political leanings, editorial boards consistently distrusted Donald Trump. Even some of those that backed the Republican nominee expressed their disdain for him but felt that they had to vote for the Republican Party platform.

It's not just the explicit endorsements, of course. It's also the implicit coverage. The mainstream media has been accused of possessing a liberal bias. But liberals *and* conservatives have castigated Donald Trump, both during the election and even now when he possesses (in theory) the presidential mantle of legitimacy.

Consider the opinion page of *The Washington Post* this last Tuesday. Liberal Catherine Rampell lays into the conspiratorial tendencies of Kellyanne Conway and crew. Liberal Richard Cohen criticizes the Trump administration's plan to replace the Affordable Care Act. Liberal Eugene Robinson excoriates the racism of Republican Rep. Steve King in the context of Trump's cozying up to white supremacists.

Fair enough: Liberals should be expected to sink their teeth into Trump.

But then there's also Jennifer Rubin, a conservative, who criticizes Trump's managerial capacities as president. Meanwhile, Michael Gerson, former speechwriter for George W. Bush, declares that "Republicans are defining lunacy down."

Voila, a full-court press on the presidency. Trump is an affront to virtually anyone, regardless of their ideology, who plays (and profits) by the rules of the game.

If I were a Trump supporter, I'd cancel my subscription to the *Post*. But I'd probably have stopped reading the newspaper and watching CNN long ago because they tend to reflect elite biases (which are sometimes but not always liberal). It's rare that the media covers labor issues or the concerns of working-class Americans these days, except to reflect on the scourge of drug addiction in the Midwest or to mourn a lost age of manufacturing. The mainstream media provides news by the bi-coastal elite and for the bi-coastal elite.

I've also had my own frustrations with the mainstream media in the United States. They did a lousy job exposing the lies the George W. Bush administration used to justify the invasion of Iraq. They didn't subject Obama's drone program to sufficient scrutiny. They betray a corporate bias. Certain parts of the world, like Africa, get precious little coverage. And so on.

The mainstream media, designed to be a watch-dog institution, certainly needs its own watch dogs, and that's where alternative media come in. But let's be clear: The mainstream media is indispensable. Media that maintain full-time reporters, foreign bureaus, and fact-checkers are an absolute requirement in a democracy. *The New York Times* and CNN can't be replaced by Internet sites and their comments sections. That way lies madness (and Breitbart).

We don't need to engage in thought experiments about what would happen if the mainstream media disappeared or if their independence were compromised. All we have to do is look at Turkey.

FIRST GO AFTER THE JOURNALISTS....

The 259 journalists in jail around the world in 2016 was the highest number since 1990. Turkey, meanwhile, leads the pack in this dubious category, with at least 81 reporters in prison (and possibly as many as 191).

Most recently, the Turkish government made headlines when it arrested Deniz Yücel, a Turkish-German journalist working for the German newspaper *Die Welt*, accusing him of being a terrorist. Yücel was actually more dangerous than a terrorist — he was part of a team investigating corruption involving the government and the family of Turkish President Recep Tayyip Erdogan.

The arrest of journalists is only part of the post-coup crackdown by Erdogan. The Turkish government has shut down 149 media outlets, dismissed over 4,000 judges and prosecutors, fired over 7,000 academics, and arrested over 40,000 people.

But Erdogan didn't just start arresting journalists after the coup attempt last July. Journalists were a primary target of Erdogan's assault on what he called the "deep state" in Turkey, which refers to at various times: the military, ultra-nationalists, pro-Gulen forces, anti-Gulen forces, and so on. (Fethullah Gulen, a one-time ally of Erdogan, is the head of an Islamic movement that maintains educational institutions all over the world, counts on many adherents within Turkey, and may or may not have been behind the July coup). The "deep state," which actually did launch several successful coups in Turkey's past, has now become convenient shorthand for any countervailing power that might oppose Erdogan, whose attacks on this subterranean creature have been an effective strategy for consolidating power.

Ominously, the Trump administration has also used this same phrase, the "deep state," though it refers to a different of characters.

The "deep state" might refer to the infamous "blob" — the foreign policy network in Washington that resisted some of Obama's more transformational efforts in international relations. It might stand in for any pro-Obama foreign policy faction that now opposes Trump. It might be another way of describing an array of government officials using bureaucratic inaction, calculated leaks, or deliberate sabotage to undermine the new administration's policies. Or it might be a much larger target that includes think tanks, media, and NGOs that aren't Trump-positive.

To defeat the "deep state," Trump has brought in people untainted by policymaking experience. It is also preparing to cut non-military government activities by a paralysis-inducing $54 billion to pay for an equally jaw-dropping Pentagon boost. Trump is playing on the deep antipathy that average Americans have toward government in general — roughly half of Democrats and a three-quarters of Republicans don't trust government — to root out any potential opposition inside the Beltway. Welcome to the deconstruction of America, Steve Bannon-style.

If Trump intends to follow Erdogan's game plan, expect to see journalists go to jail, particularly those probing into the opaque business deals of the Trump syndicate. Already, six reporters were arrested at the Inauguration Day protests and charged with felonies for participating in "rioting" (charges have since been dropped for four of the journalists).

The jailing of journalists will be a key litmus test of whether Trump is acting on his authoritarian impulses. Given the unpopularity of the media and Trump's demonization of it, such a move might not cause as much uproar as First Amendment advocates might think.

BREITBART UBER ALLES

You know the guy. He rails against the MSM (mainstream media) on websites all day long. Then he sends out a link to a *New York Times* article to prove some argument or another. If you point out the contradiction to him, he says, "Well, even a stopped clock is right twice a day."

Under normal circumstances, such curmudgeons are as much a part of a healthy democracy as celebrity hounds and Internet trolls. Vive la freedom of speech!

But these are not normal circumstances. Such curmudgeons now work in the White House. Former Breitbart News staffers who built their reputations on savaging the mainstream media and creating fake news in their place now have influential roles in the administration. Stephen Bannon is senior advisor. His protégé Julia Hahn is now a special assistant to the president. Sebastian Gorka, once the national security editor at

Breitbart and an "Islamophobic huckster," advises Trump on counter-terrorism.

Moreover, Breitbart is positioning itself as the go-to news source in the Trump era, not only reporting the news but making it, as it did recently by releasing an audio clip of House Speaker Paul Ryan dissing Trump during the campaign. It has hired new staff from *The Hill*, *Real Clear Politics*, and *The Wall Street Journal* to give the site a veneer of legitimacy. It's also planning to open bureaus in Paris and Berlin — to link up, no doubt, with fake news enthusiasts over there.

The assault on the mainstream media comes not only from the right. RT, the mouthpiece of the Russian government, has been giving space to left-leaning journalists over the years — Ed Schultz, Thom Hartmann, even Larry King. They, too, give the channel a veneer of respectability, for they are respectable voices. Although RT does engage in some real journalism, it is also a purveyor of fake news, such as the Pizzagate scandal or the spate of articles about Clinton's supposed health problems before the election. Given the right-wing character of Vladimir Putin's administration, RT and Breitbart are really just two faces of the same coin.

In this new information war, I'd like to propose a truce. The MSM, for its part, must try harder to address the concerns of those struggling to make ends meet, who are hurt by globalization, who are angry at the political, economic, and cultural elite of this country. And those who oppose Trump and all he stands for — stop treating the mainstream media as though it were the devil incarnate. Mainstream journalists will be key players in investigating, patiently and by the rules, all the abuses of the Trump administration.

If Trump calls mainstream journalists the enemy of the people, it's important for all of us to stand up and declare that we are enemies of the people, too.

I don't watch TV. And I don't watch CNN. But for the next four years, je suis CNN.

1. What does it mean to label a journalist or media source an enemy of the people?

2. How can governments use access to grant some journalists legitimacy? Is this a threat to a free press?

CONCLUSION

Relationships between the state and the press around the world are complex and nuanced. But too often journalists and publications are targeted through harmful rhetoric, censorship, or even violence. Restricting the freedom of the press can have a highly detrimental impact on governance and the public perception of those in power; without a free press to report on the goings-on of the state, the public has no recourse to find out when something unethical or illegal is being done. It is up to the citizenry to protect press freedom, a nuanced issue that reflects the many ways in which those in power can use their authority to silence dissent. This is why it is important for the public to stay aware of potential threats to the press and ways in which they can advocate for journalists' safety.

BIBLIOGRAPHY

Barett, Joshua. "Is Freedom of the Press Required for a Liberal Democracy?" *Mapping Politics*, vol. 6 Fall 2014. http://journals.library.mun.ca/ojs/index.php/MP/article/view/1411.

Benjamin, Media. "Flogging for Blogging?" *CodePink*, January 15, 2015. http://www.codepink.org/_flogging_for_blogging_official_saudi_policy_pinktank.

Bieri, Katie. "As National News Groups React, House Won't Back Down Over Press Access." *Cronkite News*, August 4, 2016. https://cronkitenews.azpbs.org/2016/04/08/20679.

Branzburg v. Hayes. United States Supreme Court, June 29, 1972.

Calvert, Clay. "Does Billionaire Funded Lawsuit Against Gawker Create Playbook for Punishing Media?" *The Conversation*, May 29, 2016. https://theconversation.com/does-billionaire-funded-lawsuit-against-gawker-create-playbook-for-punishing-press-60097.

Collins, William A. "Our Press Freedom is Under Fire." *OtherWords*, June 11, 2012. otherwords.org/our_press_freedom_is_under_fire.

Conley, Julia. "US and Worldwide Study Shows Never A More Dangerous Time to be a Journalist." *Common Dreams*, November 30, 2017. https://www.commondreams.org/news/2017/11/30/us-and-worldwide-study-shows-never-more-dangerous-time-be-journalist.

Daly, Christopher B. "How Woodrow Wilson's Propaganda Machine Changed American Journalism." *The Conversation*, April 28, 2017. https://theconversation.com/how-woodrow-wilsons-propaganda-machine-changed-american-journalism-76270.

Feffer, John. "I Am An Enemy of the People." *Foreign Policy in Focus*, March 15, 2017. http://fpif.org/i-am-an-enemy-of-the-people.

Feffer, John. "Stop the Presses." *Foreign Policy in Focus*, October 12, 2016. http://fpif.org/stop-the-presses.

Frank, Russell. "The Virginia On-Air Shootings: All Too Real," *The Conversation*, April 16, 2015. https://theconversation.com/the-virginia-on-air-shootings-all-too-real-46725.

Greco, Emily Schwartz. "No Happy Ending in Honduras." *OtherWords*, February 20, 2010. otherwords.org/no_happy_ending_in_honduras.

Mendoza-Moyers, Diego. "Coalition Calls for Release of Mexican Journalist Seeking Political Asylum in US," *Cronkite News*,

April 06, 2017. https://cronkitenews.azpbs.org/2017/04/06
/coalition-calls-for-release-of-mexican-journalist-seeking-polit-
ical-asylum-in-u-s.

Merrill, John C. "Danger to a Free Press." *Foundation for Economic
Education*, June 1, 1965. https://fee.org/articles/danger-to-a
-free-press.

Muller, Denis. "Making Media Accountable to the Public Bolsters
Press Freedom." *The Conversation*, February 3, 2015. https://the-
conversation.com/making-media-accountable-to-the-public
-bolsters-press-freedom-37156.

Near v. Minnesota. United States Supreme Court, June 1, 1931.

New York Times Co. v. United States. United States Supreme Court,
June 30, 1971.

Nieto Del Rio, Guilia McDonnell. "Deadly Words: The Spike in
Killings of Mexican Journalists." *Foreign Policy in Focus*, July 6,
2017. fpif.org/deadly-words-the-spike-in-killings-of-mexican
-journalists.

Obama, Barack. "Remarks by the President On World Press
Freedom Day." The White House Archives, May 1, 2015. https://
obamawhitehouse.archives.gov/the-press-office/2015/05/01
/remarks-president-world-press-freedom-day.

Potter, Will. "These Laws Make Me Want to Gag." *OtherWords*,
February 20, 2013. otherwords.org/these-laws-make-me-want
-to-gag.

Russell, Dean. "Freedom of the Press." Foundation for Economic
Education, April 1, 1965. https://fee.org/articles/freedom-of
-the-press.

Staff. "H. R. 2242." United States Congress, May 5, 2015. https://
www.congress.gov/bill/115th-congress/house-bill/2242.

Staff. "H. Res. 536." United States Congress, December 15, 2015.
https://www.congress.gov/bill/114th-congress/house
-resolution/536.

Staff. "Schiff, Pence Launch Congressional Caucus for Freedom
of the Press." Office of Adam Schiff, House of Representatives,
May 3, 2006. https://schiff.house.gov/news/press-releases/schiff-
pence-launch-congressional-caucus-for-freedom-of-the-press.

Staff. "S. RES. 150." United States Congress, May 3, 2017. https://
www.congress.gov/bill/115th-congress/senate-resolution/150.

CHAPTER NOTES

CHAPTER 1: WHAT THE EXPERTS SAY

"IS FREEDOM OF THE PRESS REQUIRED FOR A LIBERAL DEMOCRACY?" BY JOSHUA BARRETT

Ahmad, R. (5 February 2010). "Malaysian media shapes battleground in Anwar trial." *Reuters*. Retrieved April 10, 2014 from http://www.reuters.com/article/2010/02/05/us-malaysia-anwari-dUSTRE6140N720100205.

Bożyk, P. (2006). "Newly Industrialized Countries". Globalization and the Transformation of Foreign Economic Policy. Ashgate Publishing: United Kingdom.

Bratton, M. (1994). "Civil society and political transition in Africa." *Institute for Development Research Reports*, 11(6), 2.

Cevallos, D. (April 2014). "Media in Mexico: Freedom of the Press?" Puerto Vallarta.

Diamond, L. (1999). *Developing democracy: Toward consolidation*. John Hopkins University Press.

Diamond, L. (2002). "Thinking about hybrid regimes." *Journal of Democracy*, 13(2), 21-35.

FITA. (2006). Malaysia. *The Federation of International Trade Associations*. Retrieved April 10, 2014 from http://www.fita.org/countries/malaysia.html?ma_rubrique=cadre.

Freedom House. (2013a). *Freedom of the press 2013: Mexico*. Retrieved April 2, 2014 from http://www.freedomhouse.org/report/freedom-press/2013/mexico#. Uz7-7dw-iD4.

Freedom House. (2013b). Scores and Status 1980-2013. *Freedom of the Press*. Washington.

Huges, S., and Lawson, C. H. (2005). "Propaganda and crony capitalism. Partisan bias in Mexico Television News." *Latin American Research Review*, 39, 81-105.

Limpitlaw, J. (2011). "The role of the media and press freedom in society." In *Media Law Handbook for Southern Africa*. Republic of South Africa.

Park, D. J. (2002). "Media, democracy, and human rights in Argentina." *Journal of Communication Inquiry*, 26(3), 237-260.

PwC Economics. (2013). *World in 2050: The BRICs and beyond: Prospects, challenges and opportunities*. Retrieved April 2, 2014 from http://www.pwc.com/en_GX/gx/world2050/assets/pwc-world-in-2050-report-january-2013.pdf

Reséndiz, F. (2006). "Rinde AMLO protesta como "presidente legítimo."" *El Universal*. Mexico City.

Schleicher, I. M. (1994). *Televisa S.A. in Mexiko. Genese und jüngste Entwicklung eines kommerziellen Fernsehunternehmens im Spannungsfeld zwischen Rundfunkpolitik und Konzerninteressen*. Münster: 282.

Schneider, L. (2011). "Press freedom in Mexico. Politics and organized crime threaten independent reporting." *KAS International Reports*. 11, 39-55.

Scott, J., Hau, M. V., and Hulme, D. (2011). "Beyond the BICs: Strategies of influence in the global politics of development." *University of Manchester*. United Kingdom.

Symonds, R. (2009). "Top 200 world universities." *Times Higher Education*. London: United Kingdom.

The Economist Intelligence Unit. (2013). *Democracy index 2012. Democracy at a standstill*. Retrieved April 2, 2014 from http://pages.eiu.com/rs/eiu2/images/Democracy-Index-2012.pdf

Williams, F., and Pavlik, J. V. (1994). *The People's right to know: Media, democracy, and the information highway*. L Earlbaum Associates.

Wolfensohn, J. (2002). "The right to tell: The role of mass media in economic development." *World Bank Institute Report*. World Bank.

World Bank. (2012). *Mexico*. Retrieved April 2, 2014 from http://www.worldbank.org/en/country/mexico/overview.

CHAPTER 3: WHAT THE COURTS SAY

EXCERPT FROM *NEAR V. STATE OF MINNESOTA EX REL. OLSON*

1. Mason's Minnesota Statutes, 1927, 10123-1 to 10123-3.

2. Mason's Minn. Stats. 1927, 10112, 10113; *State v. Shippman*, 83 Minn. 441, 445, 86 N. W. 431; *State v. Minor*, 163 Minn. 109, 110, 203 N. W. 596.

3. It may also be observed that in a prosecution for libel the applicable Minnesota statute (Mason's Minn. Stats. 1927, 10112, 10113) provides that the publication is justified 'whenever the matter charged as libelous is true and was published with good motives and for justificable ends,' and also 'is excused when honestly made, in belief of its truth, and upon reasonable grounds for such belief, and consists of fair comments upon the conduct of a person in respect of public affairs.' The clause last mentioned is not found in the statute in question.

4. May, *Constitutional History of England*, vol. 2, c. IX, p. 4; De Lolme, *Commentaries on the Constitution of England*, c. IX, pp. 318, 319.

5. *See Huggonson's Case*, 2 Atk. 469; *Respublica v. Oswald*, 1 Dall. 319; *Cooper v. People*, 13 Colo. 337, 373, 22 P. 790, 6 L. R. A. 430; *Nebraska v. Rosewater*, 60 Neb. 438, 80 N. W. 353; *State v. Tugwell*, 19 Wash. 238, 52 P. 1056, 43 L. R. A. 717; *People v. Wilson*, 64 Ill. 195, 16 Am. Rep. 528; *Storey v. People*, 79 Ill. 45, 22 Am. Rep. 158; *State v. Circuit Court,* 97 Wis. 1, 72 N. W. 193, 38 L. R. A. 554, 65 Am. St. Rep. 90.

6. Chafee, *Freedom of Speech*, p. 10.

7. *See 29 Harvard Law Review*, 640.

8. See Duniway 'The Development of Freedom of the Press in Massachusetts,' p. 123; *Bancroft's History of the United States,* vol. 2, 261.

9. *Journal of the Continental Congress* (1904 Ed.) vol. I, pp. 104, 108.

10. Report on the Virginia Resolutions, *Madison's Works,* vol. iv, 544.

11. *Dailey v. Superior Court,* 112 Cal. 94, 98, 44 P. 458, 32 L. R. A. 273, 53 Am. St. Rep. 160; *Jones, Varnum & Co. v. Towsend's Adm'x,* 21 Fla. 431, 450, 58 Am. Rep. 676; *State ex rel. Liversey v. Judge,* 34 La. Ann. 741, 743; *Commonwealth v. Blanding,* 3 Pick. (Mass.) 304, 313, 15 Am. Dec. 214; *Lindsay v. Montana Federation of Labor,* 37 Mont. 264, 275, 277, 96 P. 127, 18 L. R. A. (N. S.) 707. 127 Am. St. Rep. 722; *Howell v. Bee Publishing Co.,* 100 Neb. 39, 42, 158 N. W. 358, L. R. A. 1917A, 160, Ann. Cas. 1917D, 655; *New Yorker Staats-Zeitung v. Nolan,* 89 N. J. Eq. 384, 105 A. 72; *Brandreth v. Lance,* 8 Paige (N. Y.) 24, 34 Am. Dec. 368; *New York Juvenile Guardian Society v. Roosevelt,* 7 Daly (N. Y.) 188; *Ulster Square Dealer v. Fowler,* 58 Misc. Rep. 325, 111 N. Y. S. 16; *Star Co. v. Brush,* 103 Misc. Rep. 631, 170 N. Y. S. 987; *Id.,* 104 Misc. Rep. 404, 172 N. Y. S. 320; Id., 185 App. Div. 261, 172 N. Y. S. 851; *Dopp v. Doll,* 9 Ohio Dec. 428; *Republica v. Oswald,* 1 Dall. 319, 325; *Republica V. Dennie,* 4 Yeates (Pa.) 267, 269, 2 Am. Dec. 402; Ex parte Neill, 32 Tex. Cr. R. 275, 22 S. W. 923, 40 Am. St. Rep. 776; *Mitchell v. Grand Lodge,* 56 Tex Civ. App. 306, 309, 121 S. W. 178; *Sweeney v. Baker,* 13 W. Va. 158, 182, 31 Am. Rep. 757; *Citizens Light, Heat & Power Co. v. Montgomery Light & Water Co.* (C. C.) 171 F. 553, 556; *Willis v. O'Connell (D. C.)* 231 F. 1004, 1010; *Dearborn Publishing Co. v. Fitzgerald* (D. C.) 271 F. 479, 485.

12. Madison, op. cit. p. 549.

13. The following articles appear in the last edition published, dated November 19, 1927:

'FACTS NOT THEORIES.

"I am a bosom friend of Mr. Olson,' snorted a gentleman of Yiddish blood, 'and I want to protest against your article,' and blah, blah, blah, ad infinitum, ad nauseam.

'I am not taking orders from men of Barnett faith, at least right now. There have been too many men in this city and especially those in official life, who HAVE been taking orders and suggestions from JEW GANGSTERS, therefore we HAVE Jew Gangters, practically ruling Minneapolis.

'It was buzzards of the Barnett stripe who shot down my buddy. It was Barnett gunmen who staged the assault on Samuel Shapiro. It is Jew thugs who have 'pulled' practically every robbery in this city. It was a member of the Barnett gang who shot down George Rubenstein (Ruby) while he stood in the shelter of Mose Barnett's ham-cavern on Hennepin avenue. It was Mose Barnett himself who shot down Roy Rogers on Hennepin avenue. It was at Mose Barnett's place of 'business' that the '13 dollar Jew' found a refuge while the police of New York were combing the country for him. It was a gang of Jew gunmen who boasted that for five hundred dollars they would kill any man in the city. It was Mose Barnett, a Jew, who boasted that he held the chief of police of Minneapolis in his hand-had bought and paid for him.

'It is Jewish men and women-pliant tools of the Jew gangster, Mose Barnett, who stand charged with having falsified the election records and returns in the Third ward. And it is Mose Barnett himself, who, indicted for his part in the Shapiro assault, is a fugitive from justice today.

'Practically every vendor of vile hooch, every owner of a moonshine still, every snake-faced gangster and exbryonic yegg in the Twin Cities is a JEW.

'Having these examples before me, I feel that I am justified in my refusal to take orders from a Jew who boasts that he is a 'bosom friend' of Mr. Olson.

'I find in the mail at least twice per week, letters from gentlemen of Jewish faith who advise me against 'launching an attack on the Jewish people.' These gentlemen have the cart before the house. I am launching, nor is Mr. Guilford, no attack against any race, BUT:

'When I find men of a certain race banding themselves together for the purpose of preying upon Gentile or Jew; gunmen, KILLERS, roaming our streets shooting down men against whom they have no personal grudge (or happen to have); defying OUR laws; corrupting OUR officials; assaulting business men; beating up unarmed citizens; spreading a reign of terror through every walk of life, then I say to you in all sincerity, that I refuse to back up a single step from that 'issue'-if they choose to make it so.

'If the people of Jewish faith in Minneapolis wish to avoid criticism of these vermin whom I rightfully calls 'Jews' they can easily do so BY THEMSELVES CLEANING HOUSE.

'I'm not out to cleanse Israel of the filth that clings to Israel's skirts. I'm out to 'hew to the line, let the chips fly where they may.'

'I simply state a fact when I say that ninety per cent of the crimes committed against society in this city are committed by Jew gangsters.

'It was a Jew who employed JEWS to shoot down Mr. Guilford. It was a Jew who employed a Jew to intimidate Mr. Shapiro and a Jew who employed JEWS to assault that gentleman when he refused to yield to their threats. It was a JEW who wheedled or employed Jews to manipulate the election records and returns in the Third ward in flagrant violation of law. It was a Jew who left two hundred dollars with another Jew to pay to our chief of police just before the last municipal election, and:

'It is Jew, Jew, as long as one cares to comb over the records.

'I am launching no attack against the Jewish people AS A RACE. I am merely calling attention to a FACT. And if the people of that race and faith with to rid themselves of the odium and stigma THE RODENTS OF THEIR OWN RACE HAVE BROUGHT UPON THEM, they need only to step to the front and help the decent citizens of Minneapolis rid the city of these criminal Jews.

'Either Mr. Guilford or myself stand ready to do battle for a MAN, regardless of his race, color or creed, but neither of us will step one inch out of our chosen path to avoid a fight IF the Jews want to battle.

'Both of use have some mighty loyal friends among the Jewish people but not one of them comes whining to ask that we 'lay off' criticism of Jewish gangsters and none of them who comes carping to us of their 'bosom friendship' for any public official now under our journalistic guns.'

'GIL'S (Guilford's) CHATTERBOX.

'I headed into the city on September 26th, ran across three Jews in a Chrevolet; stopped a lot of lead and won a bed for myself in St. Barnabas Hospital for six weeks. ...

'Whereupon I have withdrawn all allegiance to anything
with a hook nose that east herring. I have adopted the sparrow
as my national bird unit Davis' law enforcement league or the
K. K. K. hammers the eagle's beak out straight. So if I seem
to act crazy as I ankle down the street, bear in mind that I am
merely saluting MY national emblem.

'All of which has nothing to do with the present where-
abouts of Big Mose Barnett. Methinks he headed the local del-
egation to the new Palestine- for-Jews-only. He went ahead of
the boys so he could do a little fixing with the Yiddish chief of
police and get his twenty-five per cent of the gambling take-off.
Boys will be boys and 'ganefs' will be ganefs.'

GRAND JURIES AND DITTO.

'There are grand juries, and there are grand juries. The last
one was a real grand jury. It acted. The present one is like
the scion who is labelled 'Junior.' That means not so good.
There are a few mighty good folks on it-there are some who
smell bad. One petty peanut polician whose graft was almost
pitiful in its size when he was a public official, has already
shot his mouth off in several places. He is establishing his
alibi in advance for what he intends to keep from
taking place.

'But George, we won't bother you. (Meaning a grand
juror.) We are aware that the gambling syndicate was waiting
for your body to convene before the big crap game opened
again. The Yids has your dimensions, apparently, and we always
go by the judgment of a dog in appraising people.

'We will call for a special grand jury and a special prosecutor within a short time, as soon as half of the staff can nav-
igate to advantage, and then we'll show you what a real grand
jury can do. Up to the present we have been merely tapping on
the window. Very soon we shall start smashing glass.'

14. May, *Constitutional History of England*, c. 1X. Duniway, *Freedom
of the Press in Massachusetts*, cc. I and II; Cooley, *Constitutional
Limitations* (8th Ed.) vol. II, pp. 880, 881; Pound, *Equitable Relief
against Defamation*, 29 Harv. L. Rev. 640, 650, et seq.; Madison,
Letters and Other Writings (1865 Ed.) Vol. IV, pp. 542, 543; *Respublica v. Oswald*, 1 Dall. 319; Rawle, *A iew of the Constitution* (2d
Ed. 1829) p. 124; Paterson, *Liberty of the Press*, c. III.

15.

1. Any person who, as an individual, or as a member or employee of a firm, or association or organization, or as an officer, director, member or employee of a corporation, shall be engaged in the business of regularly or customarily producing, publishing or circulating, having in possession, selling or giving away.

    (a) an obscene, lewd and lascivious newspaper, magazine, or other periodical, or

    (b) a malicious, scandalous and defamatory newspaper, magazine or other periodical, is guilty of a nuisance, and all persons guilty of such nuisance may be enjoined, as hereinafter provided. ...

    In actions brought under (b) above, there shall be available the defense that the truth was published with good motives and for justifiable ends and in such actions the plaintiff shall not have the right to report (resort) to issues or editions of periodicals taking place more than three months before the commencement of the action.

2. Whenever any such nuisance is committed or is kept, maintained, or exists, as above provided for, the County Attorney of any county where any such periodical is published or circulated ... may commence and maintain in the District Court of said county, an action in the name of the State of Minnesota ... to perpetually enjoin the person or persons committing, conducting or maintaining any such nuisance, from further committing, conducting, or maintaining any such nuisance. ...

3. The action may be brought to trial and tried as in the case of other actions in such District Court, and shall be governed by the practice and procedure applicable to civil actions for injunctions.

    After trial the court may make its order and judgment permanently enjoining any and all defendants found guilty of violating this act from further committing or continuing the acts prohibited hereby, and in and by such judgment, such nuisance may be wholly abated.

    The court may, as in other cases of contempt, at any time punish, by fine of not more than $1,000, or by imprisonment in the county jail for not more than twelve months, any person or persons violating any injunction, temporary or permanent, made or issued pursuant to this act. Laws Minn. 1925, c. 285.

NEW YORK TIMES CO. V. UNITED STATES,
UNITED STATES SUPREME COURT

1. In introducing the Bill of Rights in the House of Representatives, Madison said:

    "[B]ut I believe that the great mass of the people who opposed [the Constitution] disliked it because it did not contain effectual provisions against the encroachments on particular rights. . . ." 1 Annals of Cong. 433.

    Congressman Goodhue added:

    "[I]t is the wish of many of our constituents that something should be added to the Constitution to secure in a stronger manner their liberties from the inroads of power." Id. at 426.

2. The other parts were:

    "The civil rights of none shall be abridged on account of religious belief or worship, nor shall any national religion be established, nor shall the full and equal rights of conscience be in any manner, or on any pretext, infringed."

    "The people shall not be restrained from peaceably assembling and consulting for their common good, nor from applying to the Legislature by petitions, or remonstrances, for redress of their grievances." 1 Annals of Cong. 434.

3. Tr. of Oral Arg. 76.

4. Brief for the United States 13-14.

5. Compare the views of the Solicitor General with those of James Madison, the author of the First Amendment. When speaking of the Bill of Rights in the House of Representatives, Madison said:

    "If they [the first ten amendments] are incorporated into the Constitution, independent tribunals of justice will consider themselves in a peculiar manner the guardians of those rights; they will be

an impenetrable bulwark against every assumption
of power in the Legislative or Executive; they will
be naturally led to resist every encroachment upon
rights expressly stipulated for in the Constitution
by the declaration of rights." 1 Annals of Cong. 439.

6. *De Jonge v. Oregon*, 299 U. S. 353, 299 U. S. 365.

7. *See Beauharnais v. Illinois*, 343 U. S. 250, 343 U. S. 267 (dissenting opinion of MR. JUSTICE BLACK), 284 (my dissenting
opinion); *Roth v. United States*, 354 U. S. 476, 354 U. S. 508 (my
dissenting opinion which MR. JUSTICE BLACK joined); *Yates
v. United States*, 354 U. S. 298, 354 U. S. 339 (separate opinion
of MR. JUSTICE BLACK which I joined); *New York Times Co.
v. Sullivan*, 376 U. S. 254,376 U. S. 293 (concurring opinion of
MR. JUSTICE BLACK which I joined); *Garrison v. Louisiana*,
379 U. S. 64, 379 U. S. 80 (my concurring opinion which MR.
JUSTICE BLACK joined).

8. These documents contain data concerning the communications
system of the United States, the publication of which is made
a crime. But the criminal sanction is not urged by the United
States as the basis of equity power.

9. There are numerous sets of this material in existence, and they
apparently are not under any controlled custody. Moreover, the
President has sent a set to the Congress. We start, then, with
a case where there already is rather wide distribution of the
material that is destined for publicity, not secrecy. I have gone
over the material listed in the in camera brief of the United
States. It is all history, not future events. None of it is more
recent than 1968.

* *Freedman v. Maryland*, 380 U. S. 51 (1965), and similar cases
regarding temporary restraints of allegedly obscene materials
are not in point. For those cases rest upon the proposition that
"obscenity is not protected by the freedoms of speech and
press." *Roth v. United States*, 354 U. S. 476, 354 U. S. 481 (1957).
Here there is no question but that the material sought to be
suppressed is within the protection of the First Amendment; the
only question is whether, notwithstanding that fact, its publication may be enjoined for a time because of the presence of an

overwhelming national interest. Similarly, copyright cases have no pertinence here: the Government is not asserting an interest in the particular form of words chosen in the documents, but is seeking to suppress the ideas expressed therein. And the copyright laws, of course, protect only the form of expression, and not the ideas expressed.

10. The President's power to make treaties and to appoint ambassadors is, of course, limited by the requirement of Art. II, § 2, of the Constitution that he obtain the advice and consent of the Senate. Article I, § 8, empowers Congress to "raise and support Armies," and "provide and maintain a Navy." And, of course, Congress alone can declare war. This power was last exercised almost 30 years ago at the inception of World War II. Since the end of that war in 1945, the Armed Forces of the United States have suffered approximately half a million casualties in various parts of the world.

11. *See Chicago & Southern Air Lines v. Waterman S.S. Corp.*, 333 U. S. 103; *Hirabayashi v. United States*, 320 U. S. 81; *United States v. Curtiss-Wright Corp.*, 299 U. S. 304; cf. *Mora v. McNamara*, 128 U.S.App.D.C. 297, 387 F.2d 862, cert. denied, 389 U. S. 934.

12. "It is quite apparent that, if, in the maintenance of our international relations, embarrassment -- perhaps serious embarrassment -- is to be avoided and success for our aims achieved, congressional legislation which is to be made effective through negotiation and inquiry within the international field must often accord to the President a degree of discretion and freedom from statutory restriction which would not be admissible were domestic affairs alone involved. Moreover, he, not Congress, has the better opportunity of knowing the conditions which prevail in foreign countries, and especially is this true in time of war. He has his confidential sources of information. He has his agents in the form of diplomatic, consular and other officials. Secrecy in respect of information gathered by them may be highly necessary, and the premature disclosure of it productive of harmful results. Indeed, so clearly is this true that the first President refused to accede to a request to lay before the House of Representatives the instructions, correspondence and documents relating to the negotiation of the Jay Treaty -- a refusal the wisdom of which was recognized by

the House itself, and has never since been doubted. . . ."
United States v. Curtiss-Wright Corp., 299 U. S. 304, 299 U. S. 320.

13. As noted elsewhere, the *Times* conducted its analysis of the 47 volumes of Government documents over a period of several months, and did so with a degree of security that a government might envy. Such security was essential, of course, to protect the enterprise from others. Meanwhile, the *Times* has copyrighted its material, and there were strong intimations in the oral argument that the Times contemplated enjoining its use by any other publisher in violation of its copyright. Paradoxically, this would afford it a protection, analogous to prior restraint, against all others -- a protection the Times denies the Government of the United States.

14. Interestingly, the *Times* explained its refusal to allow the Government to examine its own purloined documents by saying in substance this might compromise its sources and informants! The *Times* thus asserts a right to guard the secrecy of its sources while denying that the Government of the United States has that power.

15. With respect to the question of inherent power of the Executive to classify papers, records, and documents as secret, or otherwise unavailable for public exposure, and to secure aid of the courts for enforcement, there may be an analogy with respect to this Court. No statute gives this Court express power to establish and enforce the utmost security measures for the secrecy of our deliberations and records. Yet I have little doubt as to the inherent power of the Court to protect the confidentiality of its internal operations by whatever judicial measures may be required.

* The hearing in the *Post* case before Judge Gesell began at 8 a.m. on June 21, and his decision was rendered, under the hammer of a deadline imposed by the Court of Appeals, shortly before 5 p.m. on the same day. The hearing in the *Times* case before Judge Gurfein was held on June 18, and his decision was rendered on June 19. The Government's appeals in the two cases were heard by the Courts of Appeals for the District of Columbia and Second Circuits, each court sitting en banc, on June 22. Each court rendered its decision on the following afternoon.

BRANZBURG V. HAYES, UNITED STATES SUPREME COURT

1. The article contained the following paragraph:
   "'I don't know why I'm letting you do this story,' [one infor-mant] said quietly. 'To make the narcs (narcotics detectives) mad, I guess. That's the main reason.' However, Larry and his partner asked for and received a promise that their names would be changed." App. 3-4.

2. The Foreman of the grand jury reported that petitioner Branzburg had refused to answer the following two questions:
   "#1. On November 12, or 13, 1969, who was the person or persons you observed in possession of Marijuana, about which you wrote an article in the Courier-Journal on November 15, 1969?"
   "#2. On November 12, or 13, 1969, who was the person or persons you observed compounding Marijuana, producing same to a compound known as Hashish?"App. 6.

3. Judge J. Miles Pound. The respondent in this case, Hon. John P. Hayes, is the successor of Judge Pound.

4. Ky.Rev.Stat. § 421.100 provides:
   "No person shall be compelled to disclose in any legal proceeding or trial before any court, or before any grand or petit jury, or before the presiding officer of any tribunal, or his agent or agents, or before the General Assembly, or any com-mittee thereof, or before any city or county legislative body, or any committee thereof, or elsewhere, the source of any infor-mation procured or obtained by him, and published in a news-paper or by a radio or television broadcasting station by which he is engaged or employed, or with which he is connected."

5. Petitioner's Motion to Quash argued:
   "If Mr. Branzburg were required to disclose these confidences to the Grand Jury, or any other person, he would thereby destroy the relationship of trust which he presently enjoys with those in the drug culture. They would refuse to speak to him; they would become even more reluctant than they are

now to speak to any newsman; and the news media would thereby be vitally hampered in their ability to cover that views and activities of those involved in the drug culture."

"The inevitable effect of the subpoena issued to Mr. Branzburg, if it not be quashed by this Court, will be to suppress vital First Amendment freedoms of Mr. Branzburg, of the Courier Journal, of the news media, and of those involved in the drug culture by driving a wedge of distrust and silence between the news media and the drug culture. This Court should not sanction a use of its process entailing so drastic an incursion upon First Amendment freedoms in the absence of compelling Commonwealth interest in requiring Mr. Branzburg's appearance before the Grand Jury. It is insufficient merely to protect Mr. Branzburg's right to silence after he appears before the Grand Jury. This Court should totally excuse Mr. Branzburg from responding to the subpoena and even entering the Grand Jury room. Once Mr. Branzburg is required to go behind the closed doors of the Grand Jury room, his effectiveness as a reporter in these areas is totally destroyed. The secrecy that surrounds Grand Jury testimony necessarily introduces uncertainties in the minds of those who fear a betrayal of their confidences."

App. 43-44.

6. After the Kentucky Court of Appeals' decision in *Branzburg v. Meigs* was announced, petitioner filed a rehearing motion in *Branzburg v. Pound* suggesting that the court had not passed upon his First Amendment argument and calling to the court's attention the recent Ninth Circuit decision in *Caldwell v. United States*, 434 F.2d 1081 (1970). On Jan. 22, 1971, the court denied petitioner›s motion and filed an amended opinion in the case, adding a footnote, 461 S.W.2d 345, 346 n. 1, to indicate that petitioner had abandoned his First Amendment argument and elected to rely wholly on Ky.Rev.Stat. § 421.100 when he filed a Supplemental Memorandum before oral argument. In his Petition for Prohibition and Mandamus, petitioner had clearly relied on the First Amendment, and he had filed his Supplemental Memorandum in response to the State›s Memorandum in Opposition to the granting of the writs. As its title indicates, this Memorandum was complementary to petitioner›s earlier Petition, and it dealt primarily with the State›s construction of the phrase «source of any information»

in Ky.Rev.Stat. § 421.100. The passage that the Kentucky Court of Appeals cited to indicate abandonment of petitioner›s First Amendment claim is as follows:

"Thus, the controversy continues as to whether a newsman's source of information should be privileged. However, that question is not before the Court in this case. The Legislature of Kentucky has settled the issue, having decided that a newsman's source of information is to be privileged. Because of this, there is no point in citing Professor Wigmore and other authorities who speak against the grant of such a privilege. The question has been many times debated, and the Legislature has spoken. The only question before the Court is the construction of the term 'source of information' as it was intended by the Legislature."

Though the passage itself is somewhat unclear, the surrounding discussion indicates that petitioner was asserting here that the question of whether a common law privilege should be recognized was irrelevant, since the legislature had already enacted a statute. In his earlier discussion, petitioner had analyzed certain cases in which the First Amendment argument was made, but indicated that it was not necessary to reach this question if the statutory phrase "source of any information" were interpreted expansively. We do not interpret this discussion as indicating that petitioner was abandoning his First Amendment claim if the Kentucky Court of Appeals did not agree with his statutory interpretation argument, and we hold that the constitutional question in *Branzburg v. Pound* was properly preserved for review.

7. Petitioner's news films of this event were made available to the Bristol County District Attorney. App. 4.

8. The case was reported by the superior court directly to the Supreme Judicial Court for an interlocutory ruling under Mass.Gen.Laws, c. 278, § 30A and Mass.Gen.Laws, c. 231, § 111 (1959). The Supreme Judicial Court's decision appears at 358 Mass. 604, 266 N.E.2d 297 (1971).

9. "We do not have before us the text of any specific questions which Pappas has refused to answer before the grand jury, or any petition to hold him for contempt for his refusal. We have only general statements concerning (a) the inquiries of the

grand jury, and (b) the materiality of the testimony sought from Pappas. The record does not show the expected nature of his testimony or what likelihood there is of being able to obtain that testimony from persons other than news gatherers." 358 Mass. at 606-607, 266 N.E.2d at 299 (footnote omitted).

10. The court expressly declined to consider, however, appearances of newsmen before legislative or administrative bodies. *Id.* at 612 n. 10, 266 N.E.2d at 303 n. 10.

11. The court noted that "a presiding judge may consider in his discretion" the argument that the use of newsmen as witnesses is likely to result in unnecessary or burdensome use of their work product, *id.* at 614 n. 13, 266 N.E.2d at 304 n. 13, and cautioned that:
    "We do not suggest that a general investigation of mere political or group association of persons, without substantial relation to criminal events, may not be viewed by a judge in a somewhat different manner from an investigation of particular criminal events concerning which a newsman may have knowledge."
    Id at 614 n. 14, 266 N.E.2d at 304 n. 14.

12. The subpoena ordered production of
    "[n]otes and tape recordings of interviews covering the period from January 1, 1969, to date, reflecting statements made for publication by officers and spokesmen for the Black Panther Party concerning the aims and purposes of said organization and the activities of said organization, its officers, staff, personnel, and members, including specifically but not limited to interviews given by David Hilliard and Raymond 'Masai' Hewitt." App. 20.

13. *The New York Times* was granted standing to intervene as a party on the motion to quash the subpoenas. *Application of Caldwell*, 311 F.Supp. 358, 359 (ND Cal, 1970). It did not file an appeal from the District Court's contempt citation, and it did not seek certiorari here. It has filed an *amicus curiae* brief, however.

14. Respondent appealed from the District Court's April 6 denial of his motion to quash on April 17, 1970, and the Government

moved to dismiss that appeal on the ground that the order was interlocutory. On May 12, 1970, the Ninth Circuit dismissed the appeal without opinion.

15. The Government did not file a cross-appeal, and did not challenge the validity of the District Court protective order in the Court of Appeals.

16. The petition presented a single question:
"Whether a newspaper reporter who has published articles about an organization can, under the First Amendment, properly refuse to appear before a grand jury investigating possible crimes by members of that organization who have been quoted in the published articles."

GLOSSARY

adversarial—A relationship or situation marked by conflict or opposition.

ag-gag—State laws that forbid the undercover filing or photographing of activity on farms.

caucus—A conference or meeting between legislators in which a particular topic is discussed with hopes of reaching a solution.

democracy—A form of government defined by the rights of the people to choose those who govern them.

fake news—A term referring to the publishing of purposefully untrue information in order to mislead the public.

Fourth Estate—A term used to refer to the press and the press's influence on society and governance; the first three estates refer to the three branches of government.

freedom of the press—The ability for reporters and journalists to work without obstruction or infringement by the state.

media—A broad term that can refer to traditional sources of news as well as new digital platforms.

national security—The protection of the country.

obstruction—Purposeful actions meant to make the work of the press difficult by putting up barriers to access or publication.

partisanship—Disagreement or division marked by political differences of opinion.

press—Outlets that report news.

representatives—Men and women elected to govern a country, chosen by the public.

rhetoric—Language used in public speech.

transparency—Openness and honesty about what takes place, often done through the press.

watchdog—To maintain surveillance over a person, organization, or activity.

FOR MORE INFORMATION

FURTHER READING

Abrams, Floyd. *The Soul of the First Amendment*. New Haven: Yale University Press, 2017.

Boczkowski, Pablo J and C. W. Anderson (eds). *Remaking the News: Essays on the Future of Journalism Scholarship in the Digital Age*. Cambridge: MIT Press, 2017.

Hagler, Gina. *Understanding Freedom of the Press*. New York: Rosen Publishing, 2014.

Kluger, Richard. *Indelible Ink: The Trials of John Peter Zenger and the Birth of America's Free Press*. New York: WW Norton, 2016.

Lebovic, Sam. *Free Speech and Unfree News: The Paradox of Press Freedom in America*. Cambridge: Harvard University Press, 2016.

Radsch, Courtney. *Attacks on the Press: The New Face of Censorship*. New York: Bloomberg Press, 2017.

Rokutani, John. *Freedom of Speech, the Press, and Religion: The First Amendment*. New York: Enslow, 2017.

Rosenzweig, Paul, et al. *Whistleblowers, Leaks, and the Media: The First Amendment and National Security*. Chicago: American Bar Association, 2015.

Schudson, Michael. *The Rise of the Right to Know: Politics and the Culture of Transparency, 1945-1975*. Cambridge: Belknap Press, 2015.

WEBSITES

Committee to Protect Journalists (CPJ)
cpj.org
This international organization works to safeguard journalists
and the press. Its website includes information about freedom
of the press in regions around the world, as well as additional
data and research.

Freedom of the Press Association
freedom.press/about
This American organization works to defend journalism in the
twenty-first century. Its website features articles regarding
freedom of the press, fact sheets, and information about
crowdfunding campaigns.

Reporters Without Borders (RSF)
rsf.org/en
This international organization monitors censorship and threats
against the press, and its website includes the World Press
Freedom Index with a ranking of individual countries.

INDEX

ABOUT THE EDITOR

Bridey Heing is a writer and book critic based in London. She holds degrees in political science and international affairs from DePaul University and Washington University in Saint Louis. Her areas of focus are comparative politics and Iranian politics. Her master's thesis explores the evolution of populist politics and democracy in Iran since 1900. She has written about Iranian affairs, women's rights, and art and politics for publications like the *Economist*, *Hyperallergic*, and the *Times Literary Supplement*. She also writes about literature and film. She enjoys traveling, reading, and exploring museums.